ASHFORD
THROUGH TIME
Robert Turcan

AMBERLEY PUBLISHING

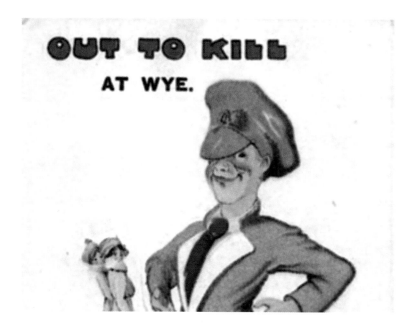

OUT TO KILL AT WYE.

Comic postcard picture of Wye.

To Robin and all the fathers of Ashford

ASHFORD'S MOTTO:
'With stronger faith' (Richard Lovelace)

First published 2012

Amberley Publishing
The Hill, Stroud
Gloucestershire, GL5 4EP

www.amberley-books.com

Copyright © Robert Turcan, 2012

The right of Robert Turcan to be identified as the
Author of this work has been asserted in accordance
with the Copyrights, Designs and Patents Act 1988.

ISBN 978 1 4456 0711 5

British Library Cataloguing in Publication Data.
A catalogue record for this book is available from
the British Library.

Typeset in 9.5pt on 12pt Celeste.
Typesetting by Amberley Publishing.
Printed in the UK.

Introduction

In Ashford nostalgia is what it used to be – a fondness for conservativeness with a small 'c' and a slower pace of life with only modest change. However, notwithstanding this the town has experienced two dramatic periods of large scale growth. The railway mania of early Victorian times that brought a network of rail track and a vast factory making trains and then after the 1960s with housing for overspill Londoners.

Its early history is linked to agriculture and the importance of its position amid productive livestock breeders. Even in the late eighteenth century the population comprised only a few thousand. Ireland, in his *History of Kent* (1830), described the town as 'pleasantly situated, the houses being mostly modern, and the High street of considerable width, the inhabitants being of genteel rank in life'. Black, in his 1886 *Guide to Kent*, waxes even more effusively. After mentioning the railway enterprises he turns to an almost poetic description: 'its High Street ascends a gentle hill, with the market-house in the centre, and St Mary's stately tower on the south, while other and inferior thoroughfares branch off on either side. At its base ripples the blithesome Stour, spanned by a stone bridge of four arches. All around spreads a pleasant country, abounding in leafy woods, broad meadows, and noble corn-fields- failing, it is true in elevation and grandeur of scenery, but nevertheless an agreeable and fertile landscape.'

Ashford is today a modern bustling town with achingly inappropriate architectural styles that somehow reflect its schism from Georgian provincialism to European business centre of the future. Targets for housing growth are so ambitious that development estates will continue to spread ever outwards to cover farmland and engulf sleepy villages.

Politically its inhabitants have traditionally had an independence of mind. Historically its most notable and rebellious citizen was Jack Cade. In 1450 he led a 5,000 strong army of insurgents against London.

Henry VI fled to Warwick, but law and order was restored after the rebels' defeat at the Battle of London Bridge and Cade's subsequent death in a skirmish. The mood of violent dissent is best illustrated by the famous quote from Shakespeare's play *Henry VI* when Dick the butcher of Ashford said to Jack Cade, 'The first thing we do, let's kill all the lawyers.' During the Civil War, Ashford generally supported the Puritan cause.

The advent of the High Speed Rail Link has heralded another phase of growth which has seen large scale construction of shopping malls, industrial estates and road improvements. Enhanced motorway links have had similar economic affects.

To place Ashford in a more comprehensive geographical context a good sample of images from surrounding villages have been included in this book. Two stately mansions namely Goddington and Eastwell are represented.

The range or variety of topics is, however, so large that the selection of images old and new is by its nature a personal choice. Nonetheless, they provide an insight into how this corner of Kent has coped with the ever present pressure need for different means of transport, shops, occupations and housing in the past century.

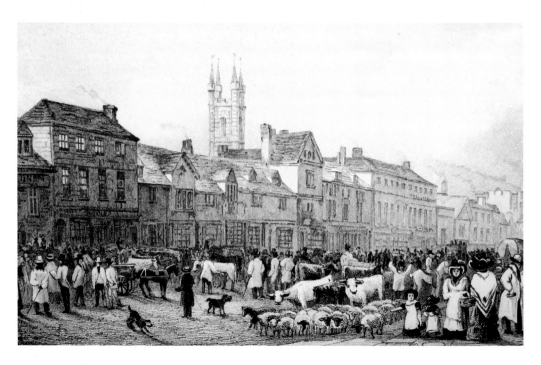

Picture of Ashford from eighteenth-century print.

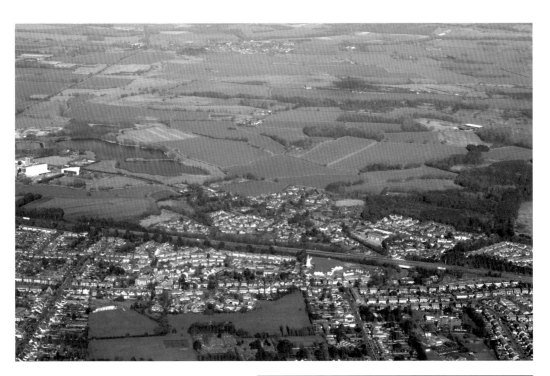

Willesborough Windmill

Flying over Ashford from the south-east, Willesborough windmill stands out as a white speck against the surrounding houses and lush Kent countryside. Close up it sits atop a knoll in first class state of repair adjacent to a museum of Norman motorcycles, which were manufactured at Ashford.

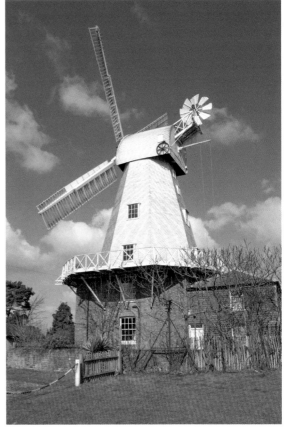

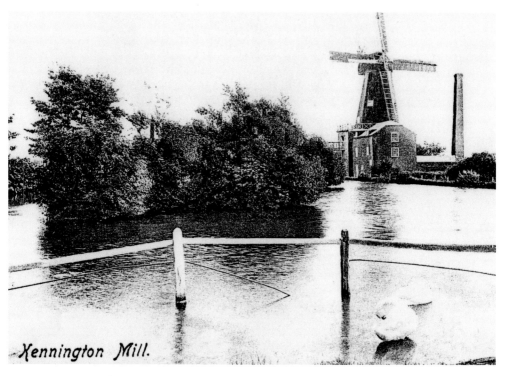

Kennington Mill.

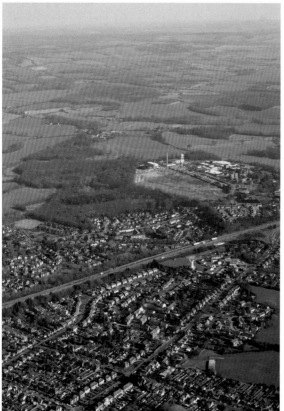

Kennington Mill

Little is left of Kennington mill but it was unique in being powered by three types of motive force, namely wind, water and steam. The pond in the picture below has gone, but a stream fed from the lake at Eastwell House remains. Kennington was once a separate settlement to Ashford, but has been incorporated into its northern boundaries on the other side of the M20 motorway. This aerial shot that was taken soon after the one on page 5 shows a distant vista of the large William Harvey hospital with its prominent water tower.

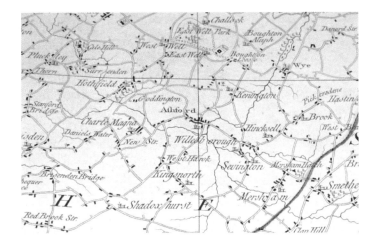

Ashford's Development over the Centuries

Few towns are better known for their spurts of sudden growth than Ashford. Originally a modest agrarian market centre with buildings lining the main street as shown in the map of 1794, it rapidly expanded with the coming of the Southern Railway line from London to Dover in the early 1840s. Industry and employment growth took off with the decision to establish a major factory for the production of steam locomotives and rolling stock. Other industries such as motor cycle manufacture, food preparation and garment makers also boosted the economy and the population grew accordingly as shown in the map of around fifty years ago. From the decision to relocate Londoners to Ashford over a generation ago, the town continues to have well above average plans for urban growth and more of the green areas on the latest map will soon change to a different hue.

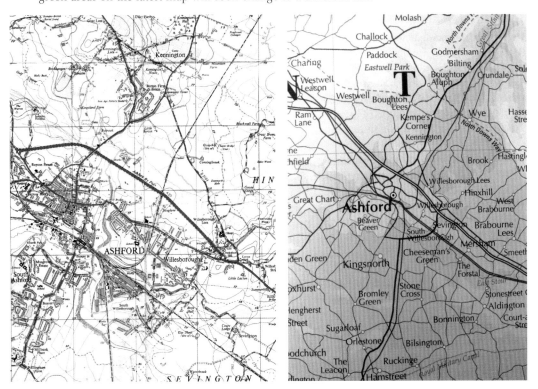

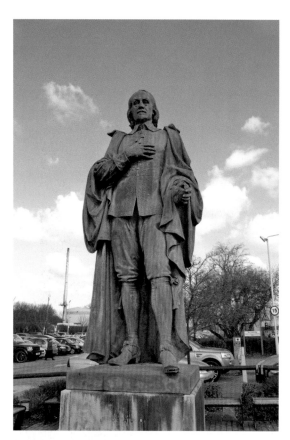

William Harvey Hospital

The William Harvey hospital is Ashford's main medical centre. It is named after William Harvey who was the first to discover the circulatory system of blood. Outside the main entrance is a statue of this pioneer from nearby Folkestone clutching a heart in his left hand.

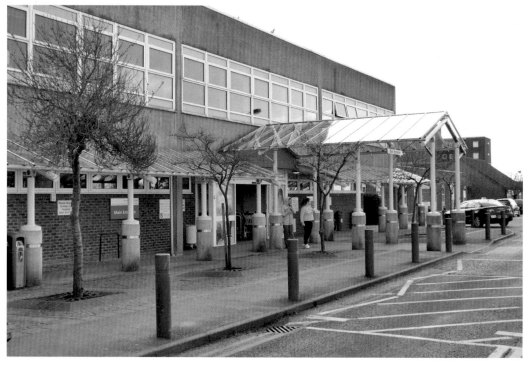

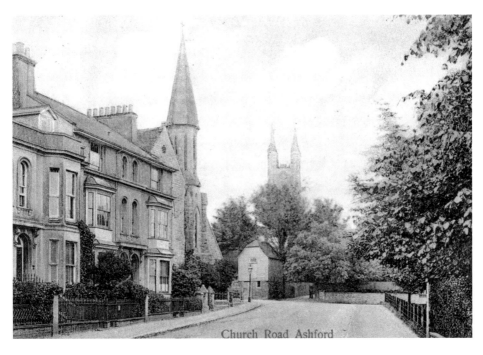

Church Road I
This street is now partly a misnomer as the more recent Victorian church on the corner has been demolished and replaced with modern offices.

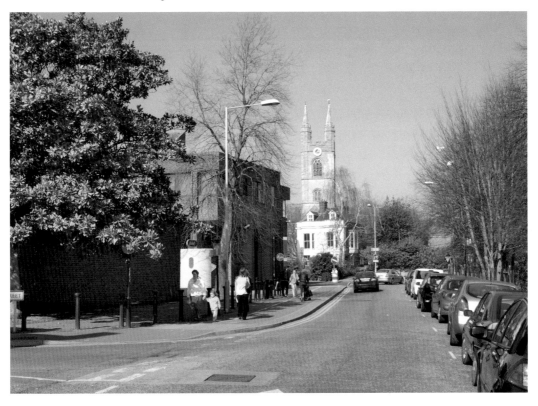

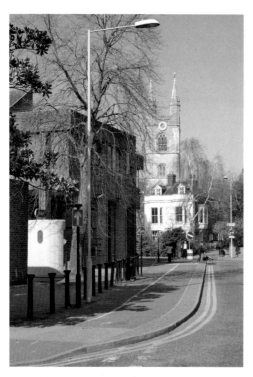

Church Road II
This monochrome portrait postcard of Church Road shows considerable differences to front elevation of the villa near St Mary's church. A nice period feature is the parked baker's delivery vehicle.

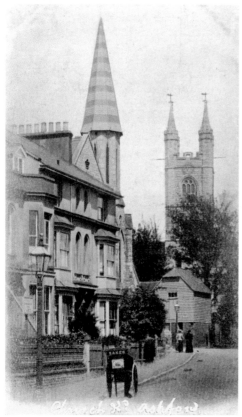

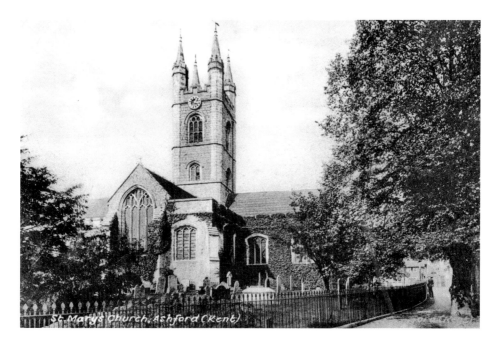

St Mary's Church I

A central focal reference point of Ashford is its stunning medieval church. Much adapted over the centuries for the town's growing needs, it provides a warm welcome to visitors in every sense. Its current caretakers have installed a heating system which derives warmth from deep below ground and enhanced seating arrangements to accommodate audiences and congregations alike.

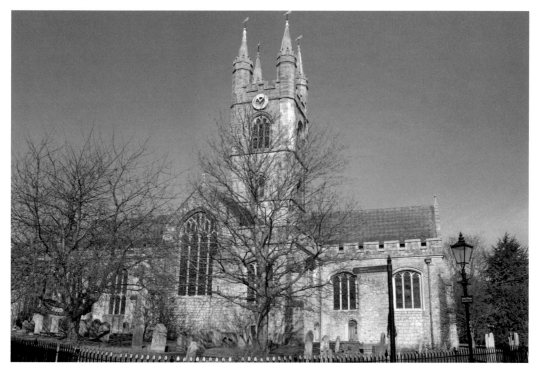

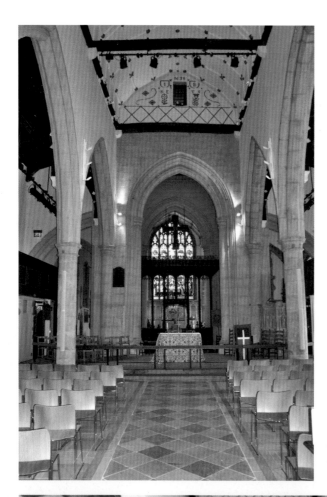

St Mary's Church II
Just as spectacular as its exterior turrets and well maintained exterior is the internal fabric of St Mary's. Beautiful tombs to long departed Tudor local worthies are subtly lit by vibrant shafts of light from coloured glass windows.

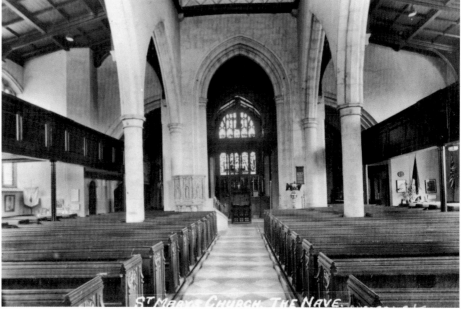

ST MARYS CHURCH THE NAVE

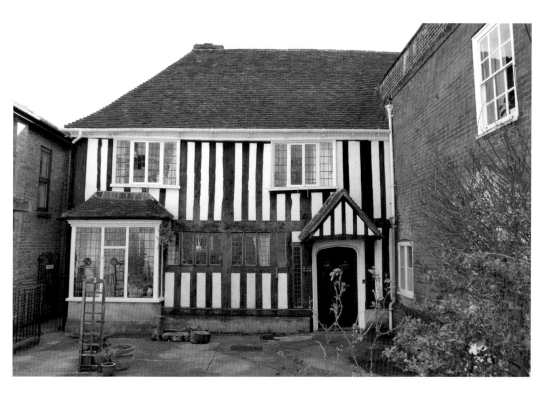

The College

Now the Vicarage this building was once part of a college for priests. Sir John Fogge of Repton, the powerful friend of Edward IV, spent a great deal of money on rebuilding Ashford church and he planned to complete this building scheme with an ancillary establishment for religious trainees.

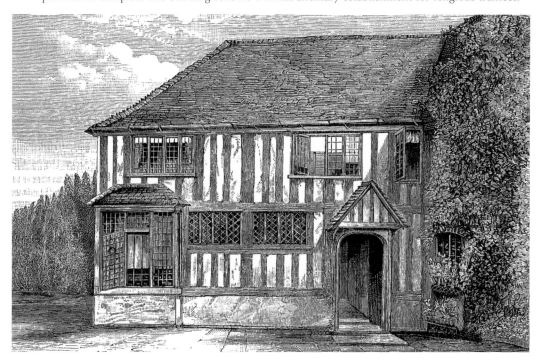

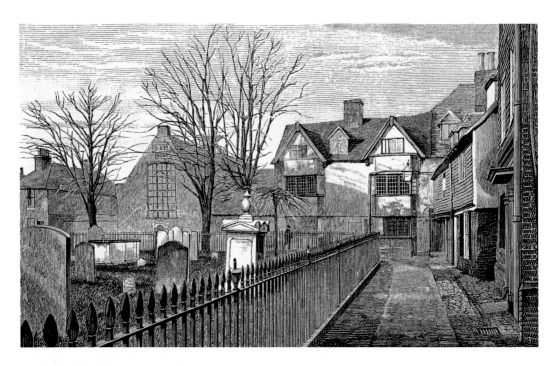

Doctor Wilks' Memorial School

Now a museum this building was originally a grammar school. It was endowed by Sir Norton Knatchbull of Mersham-le-Hatch in 1635. Many interesting period features remain inside and out including masters' and pupils' fittings, large windows and a churchlike roof. It derives its present name from a much-esteemed past doctor of the town.

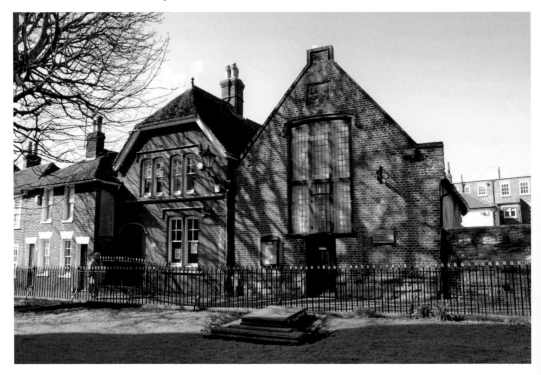

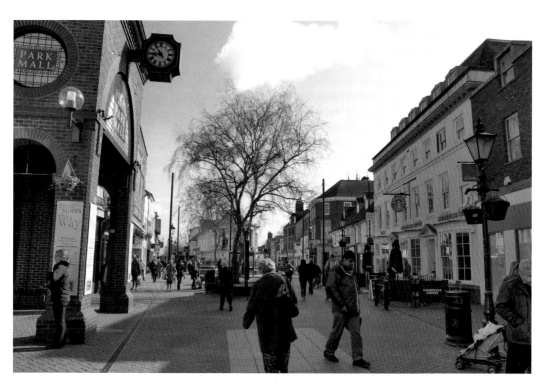

High Street

The 1930s picture below shows the upper High Street before closure for traffic. The current scene illustrates how pedestrians can freely wander around this shopping precinct. The old council buildings are now obscured by ornamental trees.

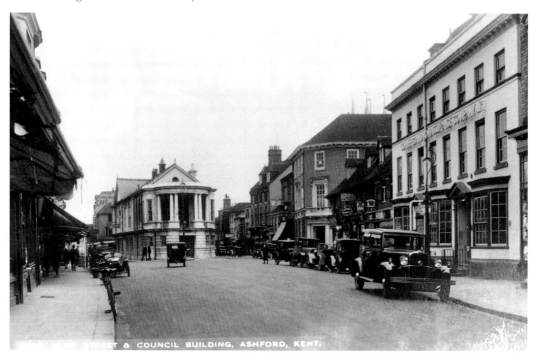

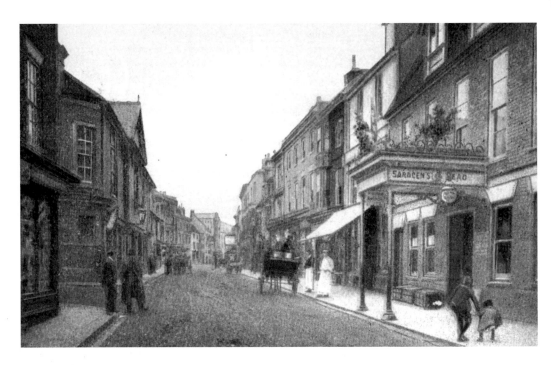

Saracens Head I

Once the social Mecca of Ashford, the Saracens Head also doubled as a magistrates' court, however sadly all vestiges of its former glory have been removed. Its original structure was of great antiquity, but it was rebuilt in mid-Victorian times. It was demolished in the late 1960s to be replaced firstly by a Sainsbury's branch and then by Boots the chemist.

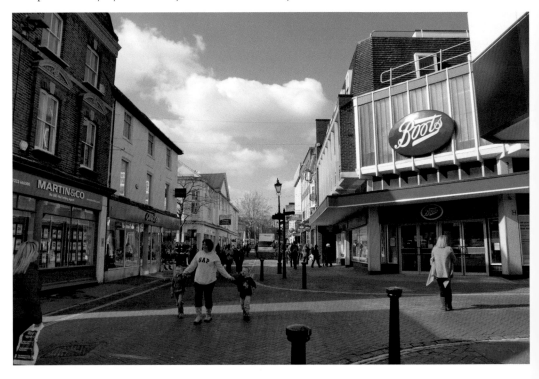

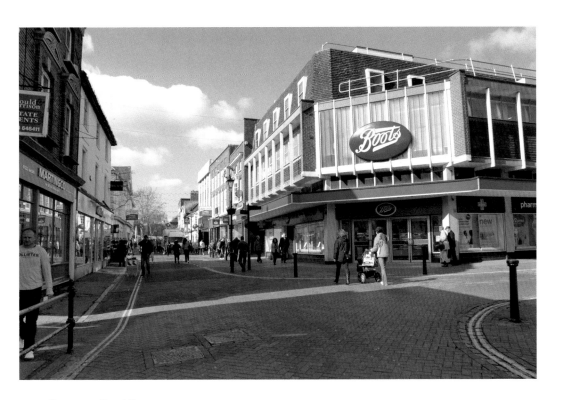

Saracens Head II

Without large scale car ownership Edwardian townsfolk similarly enjoyed unencumbered access to the High Street near this juncture with North Street. Disastrous town planning decisions on clashes of architectural styles, however, had yet to damage their built environment.

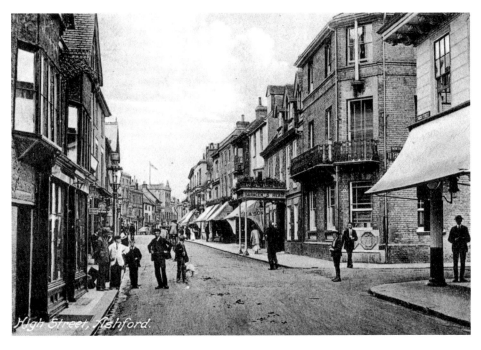

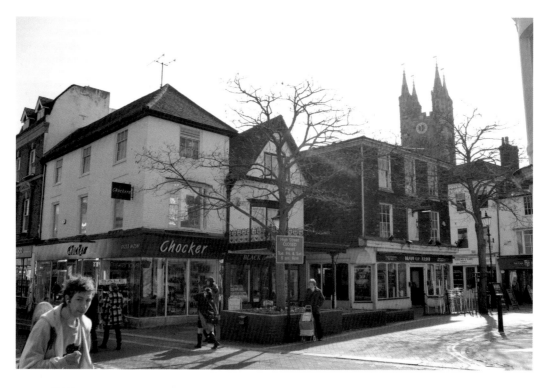

Middle Row

At the core of Ashford is this varied group of period shops. They give a good insight into the Georgian character of this market town before the onslaught of industrialisation. Only cosmetic changes to exterior decoration have taken place, but a lovely relaxed atmosphere can be gauged from the parked horse-drawn vehicles of yesteryear.

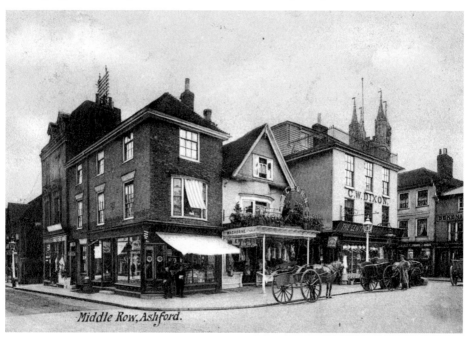

Middle Row, Ashford.

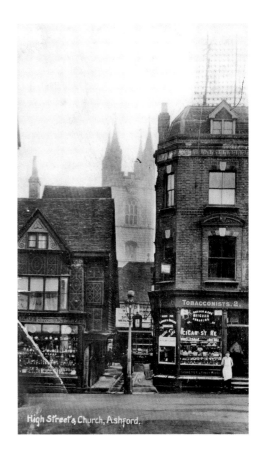

Market Place I
Tobacconist's and other retailers have been replaced by estate agent's in this corner of the main thoroughfare.

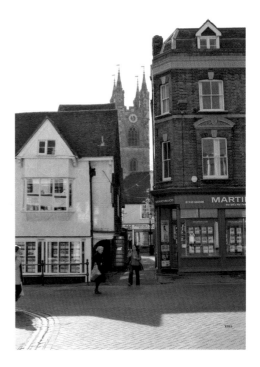

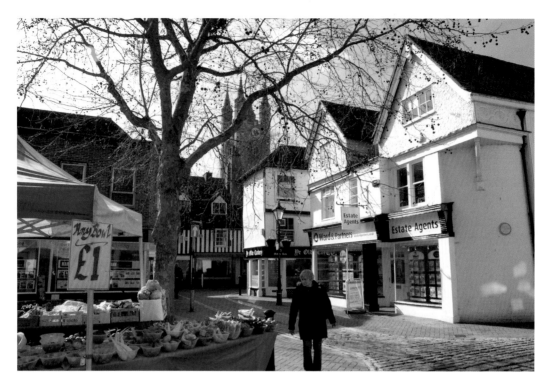

Market Place II

The monumental centrepiece behind the turn of the century school boy wearing a then fashionable Eton collar has gone. However, the spirit of this market place continues with stalls selling fresh produce.

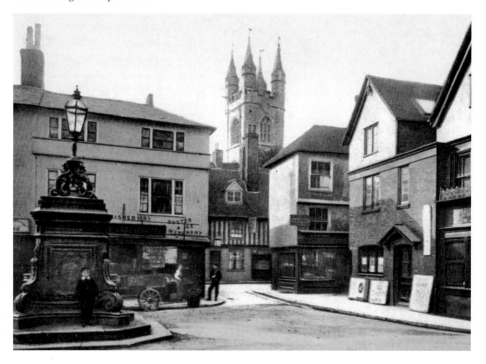

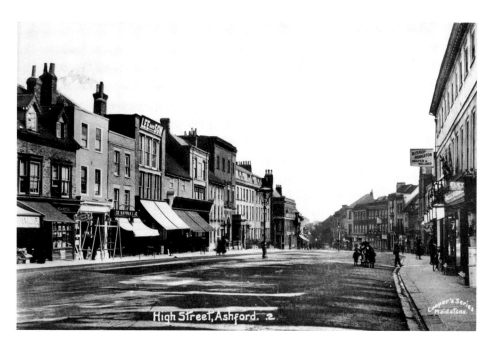

High Street I
Renowned for its width this area of the High Street once served as its livestock market. Now it is inaccessible to normal traffic, dotted with trees and a monument to a Continental twin town association.

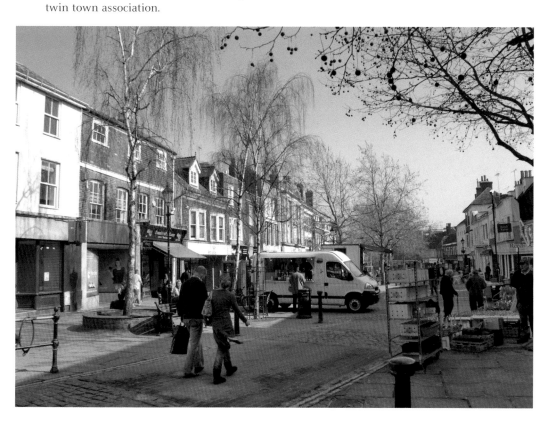

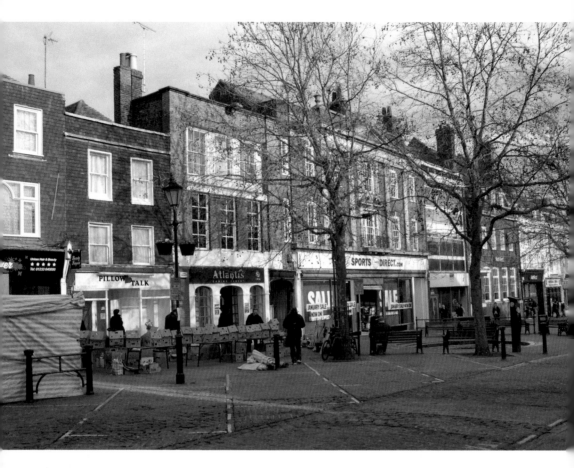

High Street II

Before shopping malls the High Street was the main trading area. The 1930s snapshot of the northern side of the upper High Street teems with consumers and their bicycles. Today a large proportion of buyers are drawn to outlets nearer convenient car parks. This is illustrated by the quieter scene above in the current lower north side on the same central erstwhile highway.

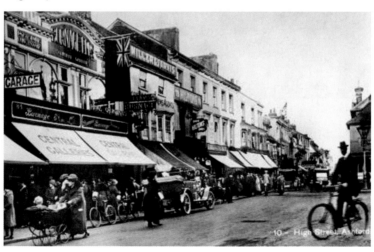

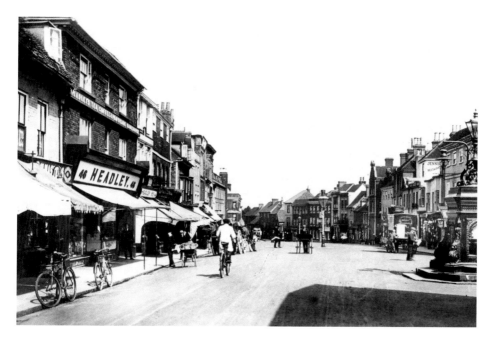

High Street III

Looking eastwards the cameraman taking the photograph above has captured the expansive nature of the road in about 1900. Well known retailers such as Headly are highlighted by their conspicuous facia board. Today a more intimate atmosphere pervades with well placed outdoor seating and flower beds.

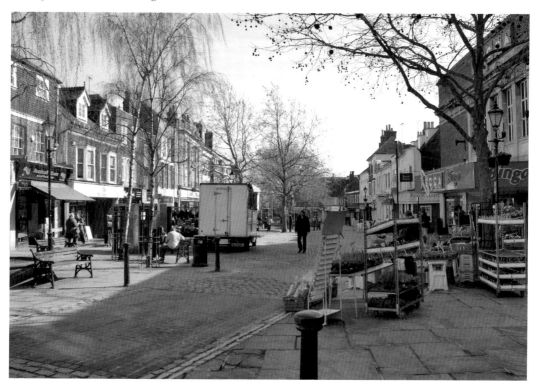

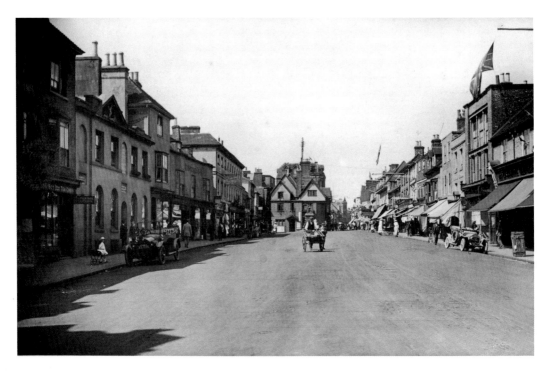

High Street IV

Two different angles and different periods are illustrated in these old pictures. Nonetheless they reinforce the wide-open character previously described before the modern day pedestrian scheme was to revolutionise the appearance of the heart of Ashford.

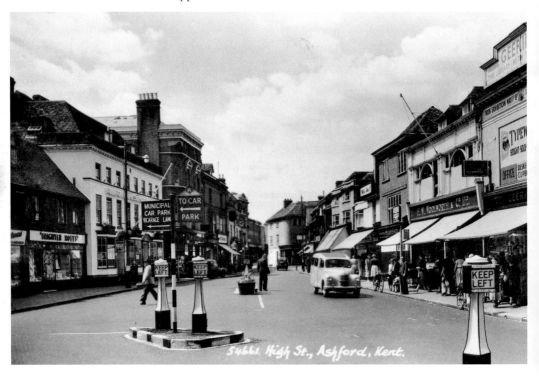

54661. High St., Ashford, Kent.

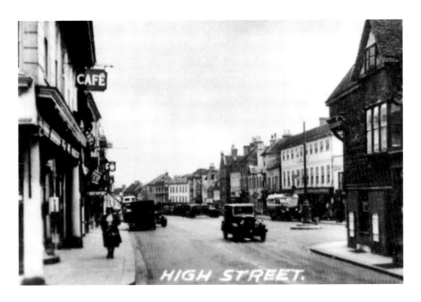

High Street V

Even in pre-war days car ownership was reserved for the more affluent minority and so indiscriminate parking in the High Street was completely unrestricted as can be seen from the picture above. Below, wider pavements fail to attract greater masses of people.

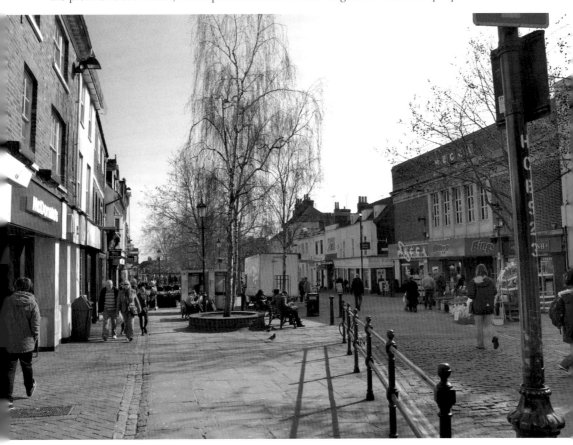

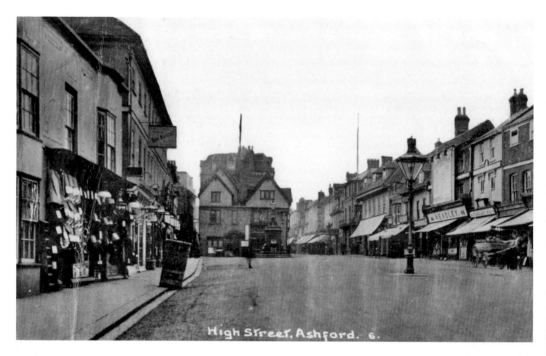

High Street VI

Canvas awnings were a virtually universal fitment to emporiums of a hundred years ago. They were designed to protect shop window displays of goods from potentially fading affects of sunlight and to shelter shoppers from the elements. The scene below is a weak echo of this phenomenon with only a temporary butcher's and small tented pavilion visible.

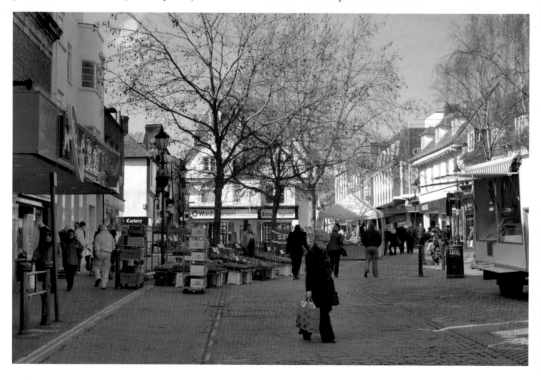

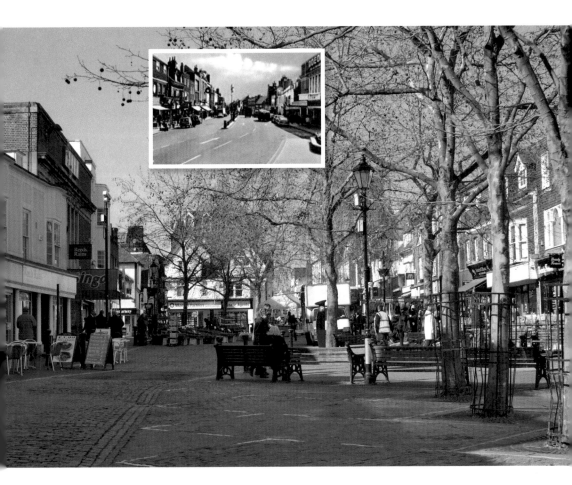

High Street VII

This somewhat fuzzy picture seen inset shows subtle changes to the street scene of the 1960s. A central road division is visible and it was still possible to go to the cinema at the nearby Odeon. Today, florist stalls reflect an almost village green pace of life to this place which has evolved from a cattle market, to a busy shopping highway to finally end up as a leisurely amenity area.

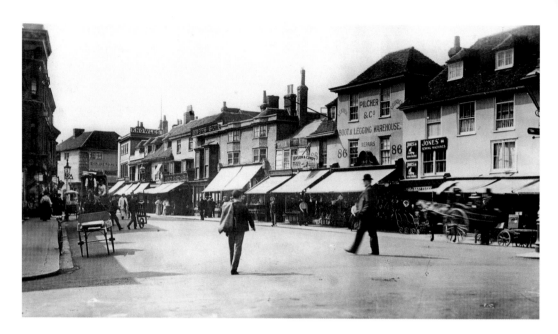

Upper High Street

Formality of clothing a century ago is well depicted in these two evocative pictures. The old boys about their business above are both wearing bowler hats as are the all male participants aboard an outing bus below. It is extraordinary that this type of hat, designed for an aristocrat's gamekeepers, should have become *de rigueur* for a whole swathe of respectable middle class gentlemen.

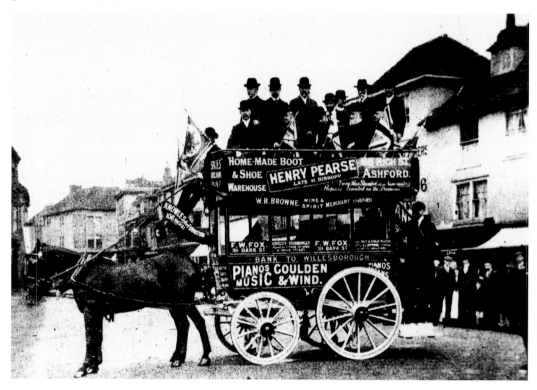

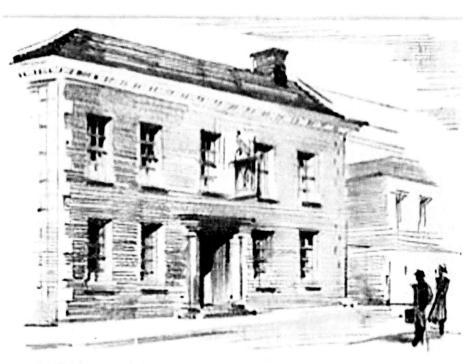

THE COUNTY HOTEL,
ASHFORD, KENT.

TELEPHONE : ASHFORD

The County Hotel

The ill-defined artist's impression above was used as a commercial advertising card for the County Hotel. However, it serves to show how this hostelry looked before enlargement with a second storey.

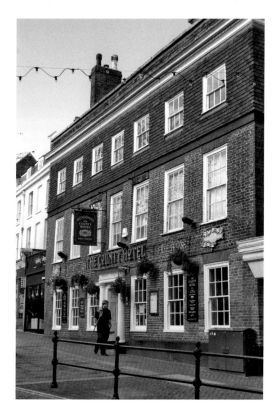

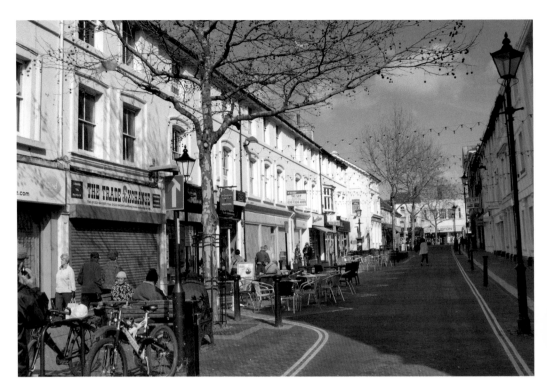

Bank Street I

Bank Street is so named because of its location for a large bank. Much of its old Victorian architecture has survived, but it is now much narrower in places to allow for the tables and chairs of boulevardiers.

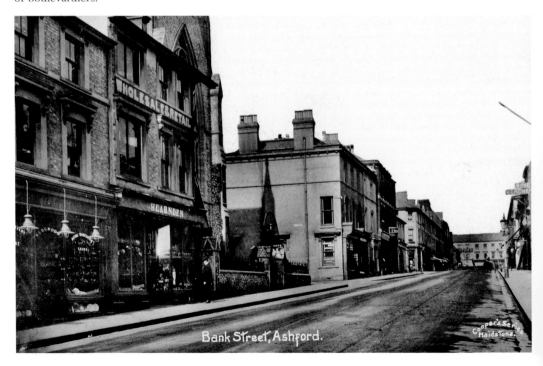

Bank Street, Ashford.

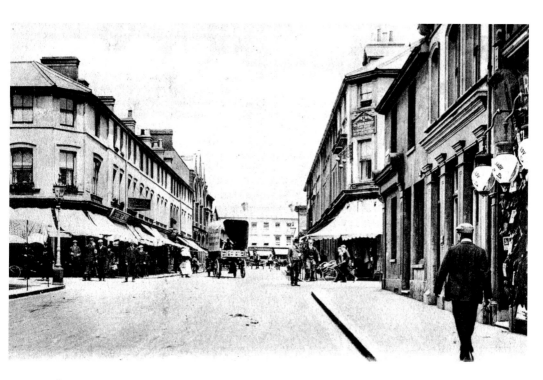

Bank Street II
There is virtually no change in these elegant terraces except that they are now painted white and the main traffic today consists of buses rather than horse-drawn carts.

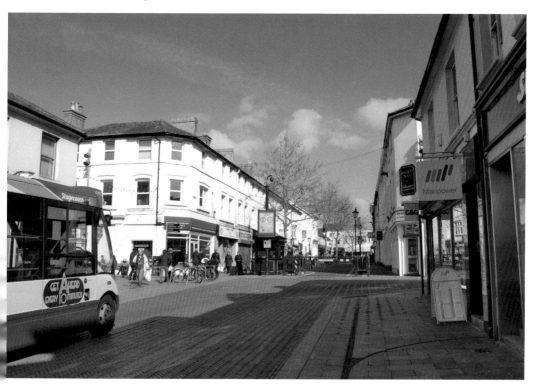

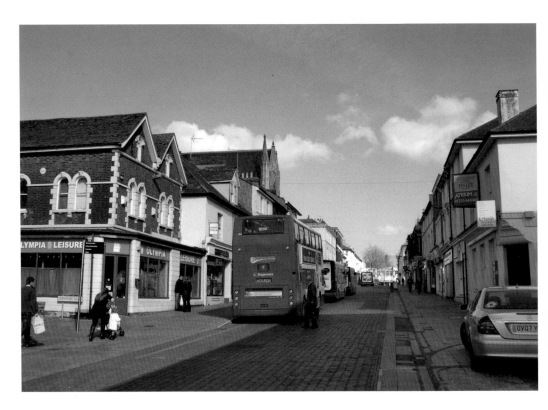

Bank Street III

These pictures reinforce the previous page's theme of little architectural change in this part of Bank Street. In particular the church and the buildings with Lombardy arched windows on the left remain virtually intact. Moreover, it can be further observed that large motorised buses have superseded draft horses and their carriages.

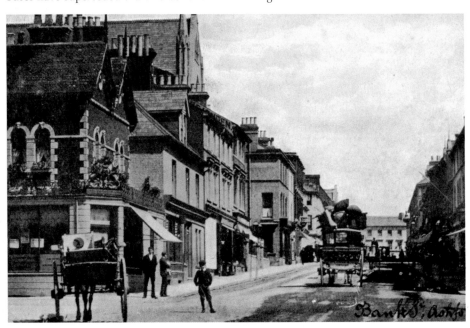

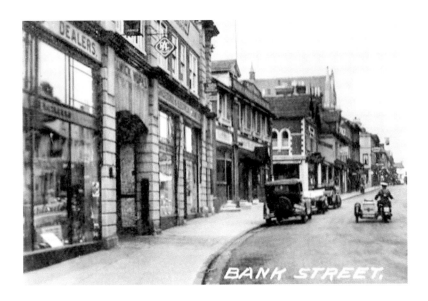

Bank Street IV

Few pictures as these can better depict the scale and alacrity of Ashford's more recent changes. The garage has been replaced by a branch of Debenhams. The contrast in design could not be more extreme with the sinuous arched pseudo art deco lines of the new building replacing the mock grandeur of 1930s respectability and substance.

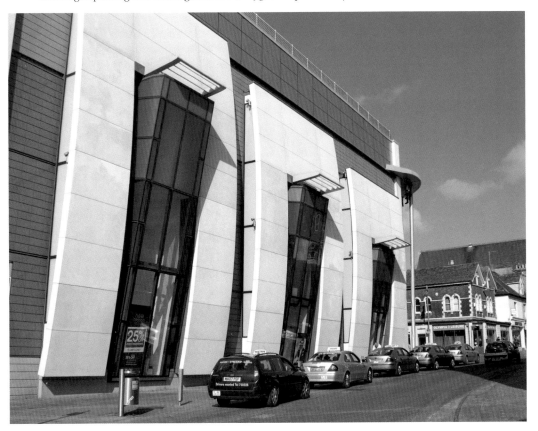

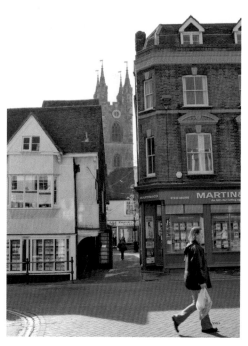

North Street I

There have been few changes to this end of North Street except for the cataclysmic alterations mentioned previously with the removal of the Saracens Head. As in Bank Street the present fashion is to paint stucco rendering white.

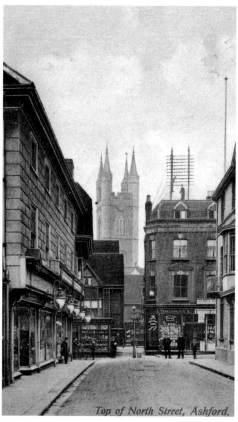

Top of North Street, Ashford.

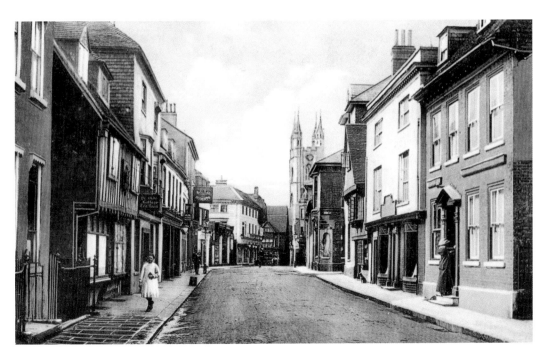

North Street II
Despite modern intrusions the overall mood of this street is medieval and intimate. Georgian façades often cover timber-framed structures of older periods.

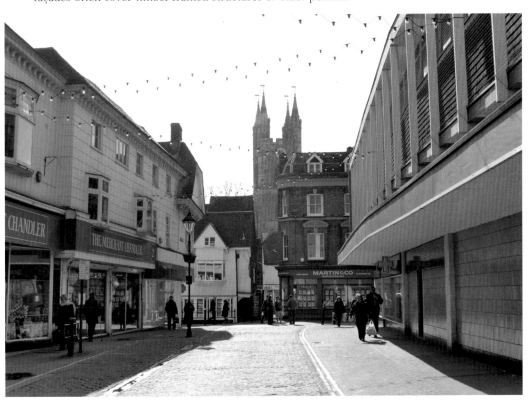

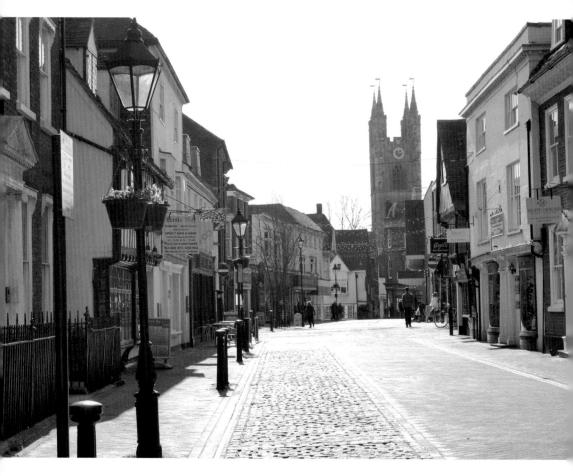

North Street III
The cobbles and ghostliness of the photograph above further emphasises the timelessness of this ancient roadway. From almost every angle the miniature spires of St Mary's tower can be seen stretching up to the skyline.

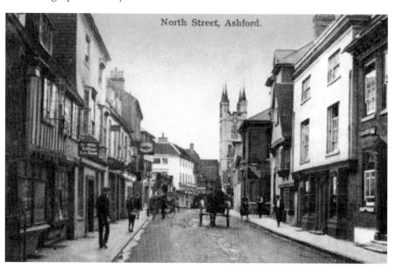

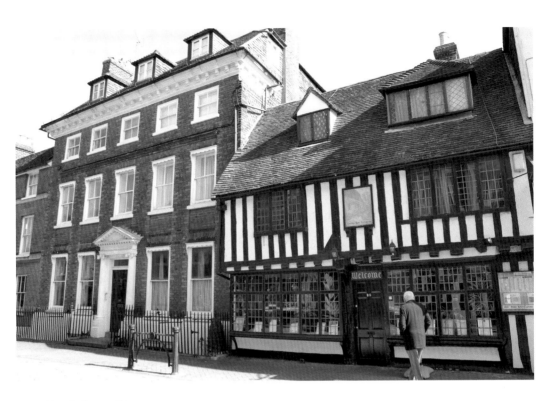

North Street IV

Beautiful period properties grace the outer end of North Street. They are in immaculate condition and their gracefulness has been appreciated by the architects who have office bases here.

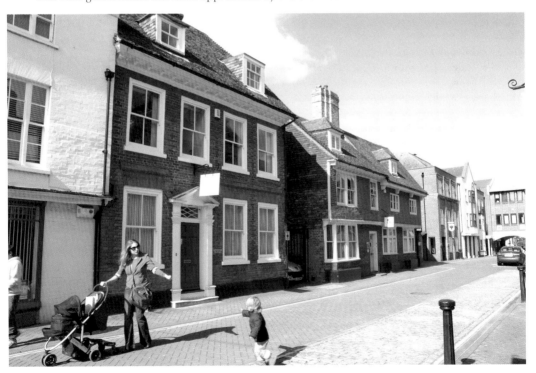

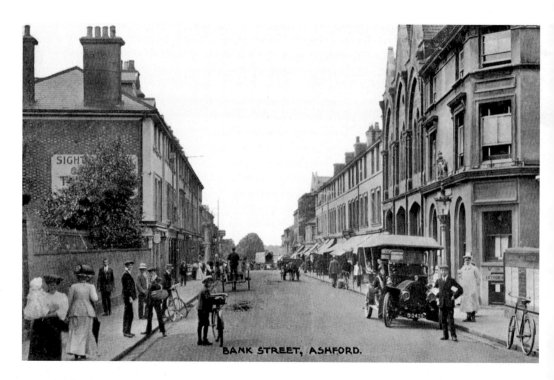

BANK STREET, ASHFORD.

Ashford Motoring Then and Now

The iconic and much-loved postcard image taken in Bank Street depicts an Edwardian veteran car parked proudly next to its chauffeur who is resplendent in calf length mackintosh and peaked cap. In contrast, a highly-polished recently manufactured 4x4 stands close to where its predecessor once was. Despite all terrain ability, only a small number of these cars ever feel the softness of grass and mud beneath their shiny wheels. Perhaps future generations will remark upon this anomalous cult following.

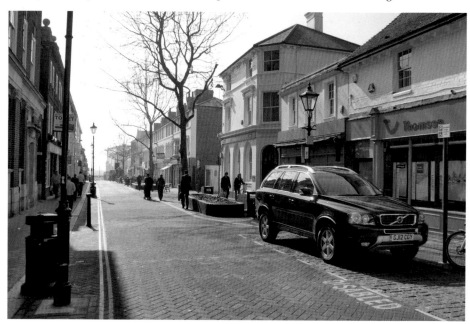

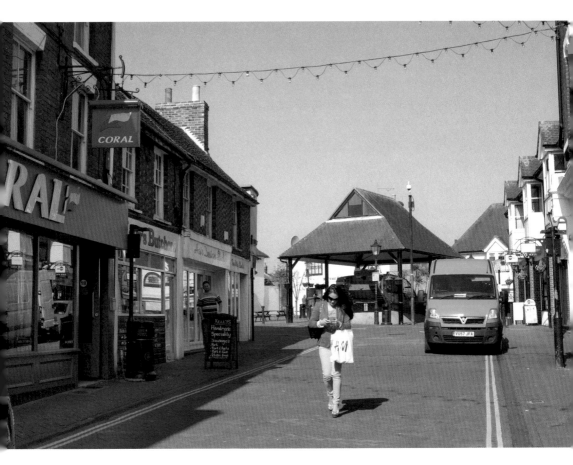

Castle Street

If the picture above is typical of Castle Street, parking still does not present a problem – despite double yellow lines. Coral bookmakers, however, have replaced what appears to have once been a greengrocer's.

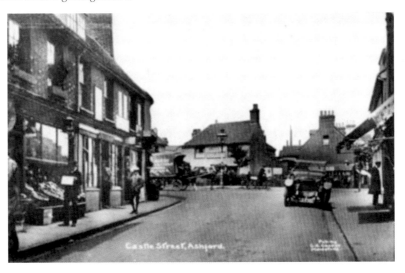

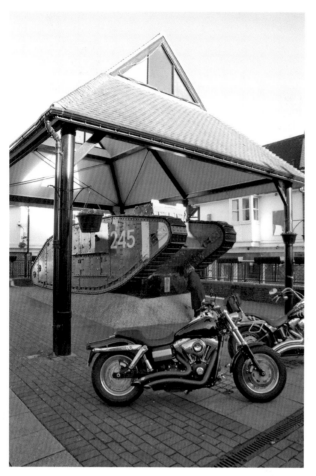

Tank Castle Street
The City of Lincoln presented Ashford with this First World War tank in 1919 in recognition of its contribution to victory. It puffed its way to its final resting place amidst clouds of burnt fuel smoke and jostling crowds. For better protection of this rare military relic a shelter has been erected overhead.

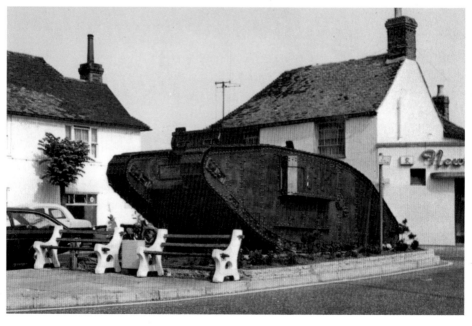

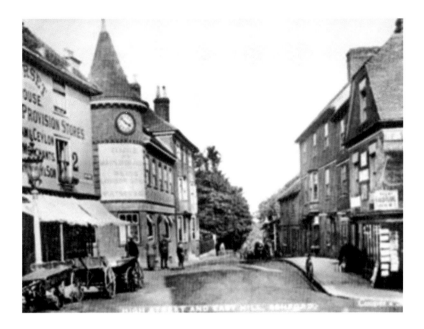

East Hill

East Hill was once a continuation of the High Street where it crossed Station Road and was the main highway from Ashford to Folkestone. As the picture below shows, access for vehicular traffic has since been blocked. Ashford School has premises here and lower down a flour mill once operated with power generated by the flowing river Stour.

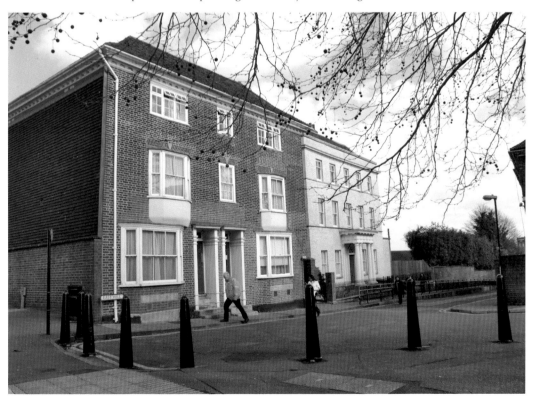

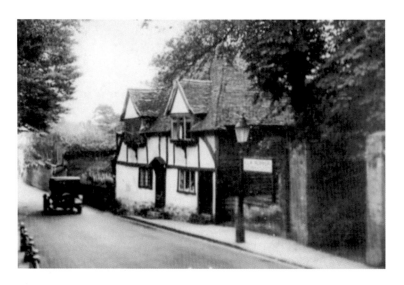

Lost Cottage East Hill
The frequently photographed black and white cottage above can no longer be located and is presumed to have been demolished. However, the descending courses of a nearby brick wall remain *in situ*.

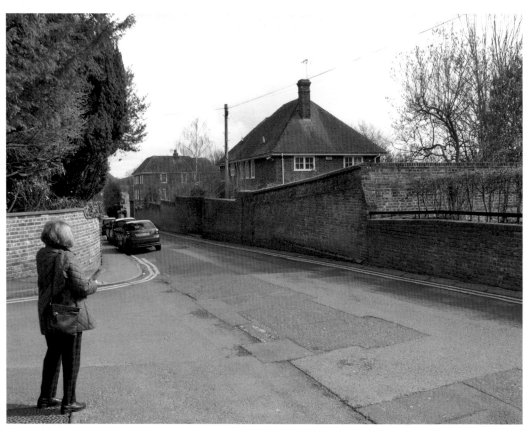

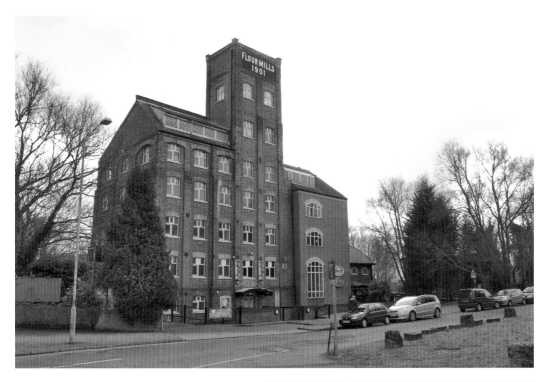

Flour Mill and Night Club

A perfect alternative use for the flour mill at East Hill has been found in the guise of a night club. The powerful race which drove the grinding mechanism is now the soothing background noise for revellers drinking *al fresco*.

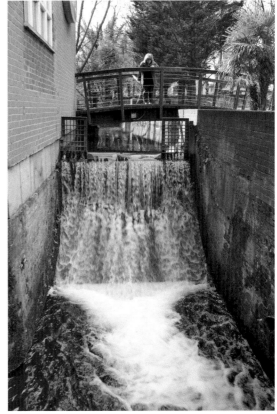

43

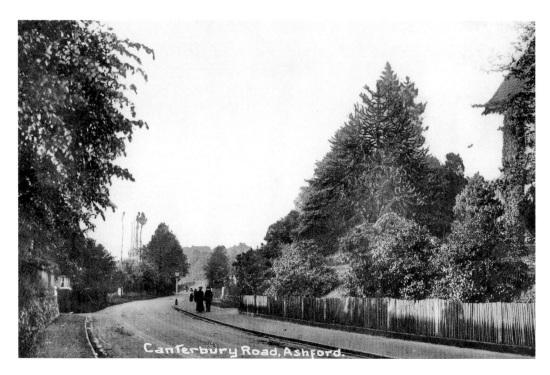

Canterbury Road

Two different aspects of Canterbury Road can be observed from these Edwardian pictures. Fine villas gradually encroached out into the surrounding countryside as the affluence of Ashford's middle classes sought residential expression.

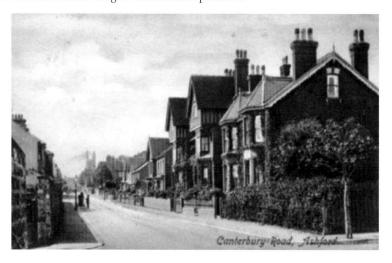

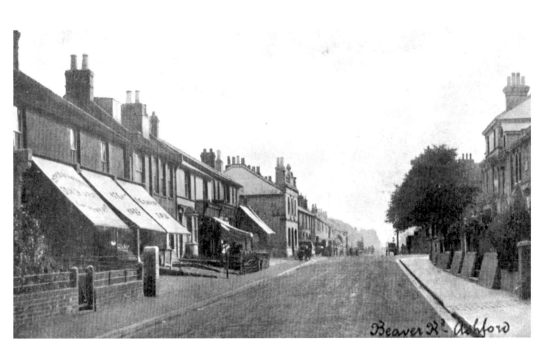

Beaver Road

Beaver Road was developed on the southerly low-lying land near the River Stour to house mainly railway factory workers who toiled at the nearby Southern Railway Works. Its substantially built houses have altered little from the outside, but internally are transformed with central heating systems, fitted kitchens and up-to-date bathrooms. There is controversy over whether one of these homes was where Sir Malcolm Sargent, the late conductor of Promenade Concert fame, was born.

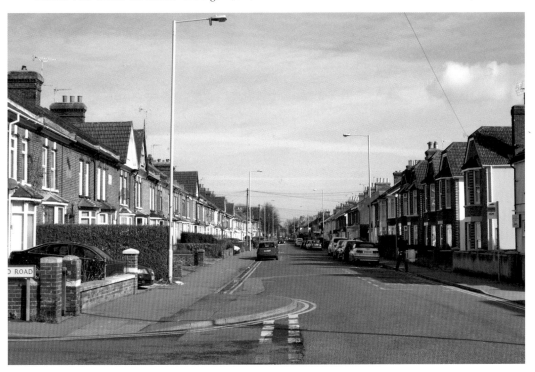

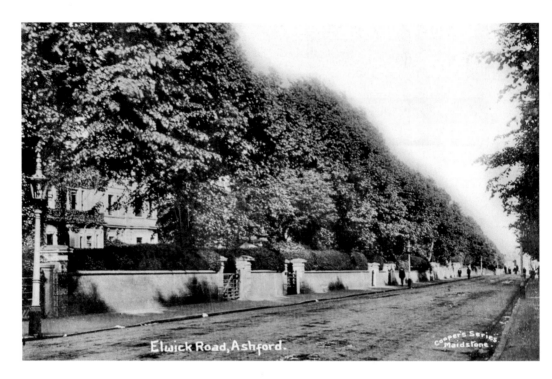

Elwick Road, Ashford.

Cooper's Series
Maidstone.

Elwick Road I

Elwick Road was named after George Elwick Jemmett, who was Lord of the Manor and owned much land on this southern side of Ashford. This family were responsible for extensive development in Ashford in Victorian times. They owned Jemmett's Bank and were instrumental in the cattle market moving to a new site off Elwick Road.

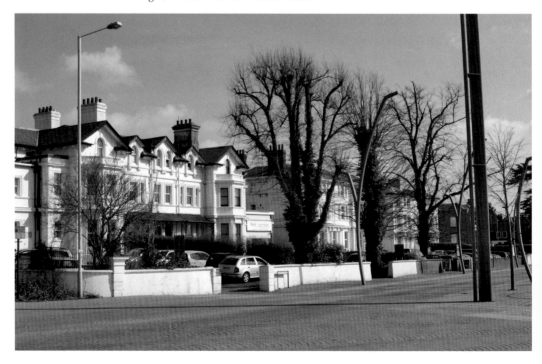

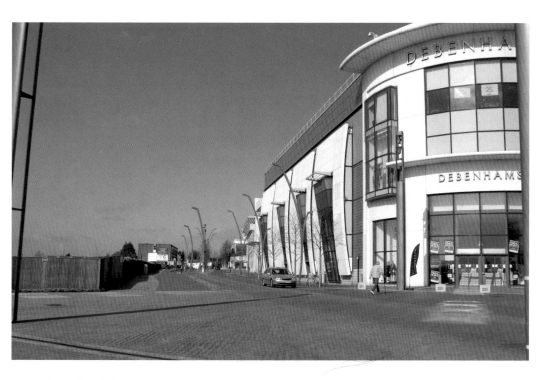

Elwick Road II

The western length of Elwick Road has been extensively redeveloped. The so-called 'shared way' which allows two-way traffic and supersedes the controversial ringway of 1970 is deserted in the snapshot above. The principal for this evolvement is to reduce any constraint on the centre of Ashford growing proportionately to meet the needs of exponential population increase. However, it seems for the moment that both pedestrians and motorists are wary of this new arrangement.

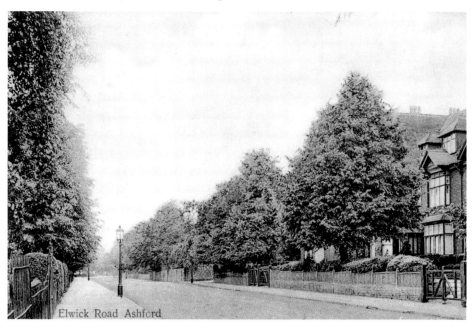

Elwick Road Ashford

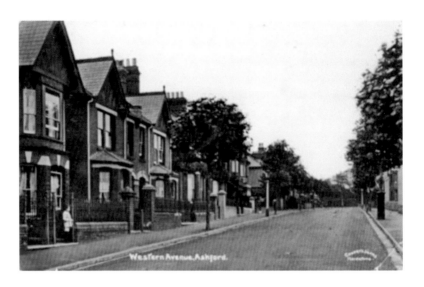

Western Avenue

Western Avenue is typical of many roads which became residential areas around the time Ashford was a booming railway town. These two photographs show that its respectable environs are little changed over the past hundred years.

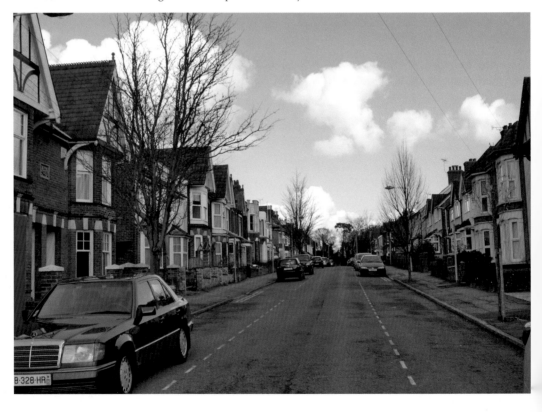

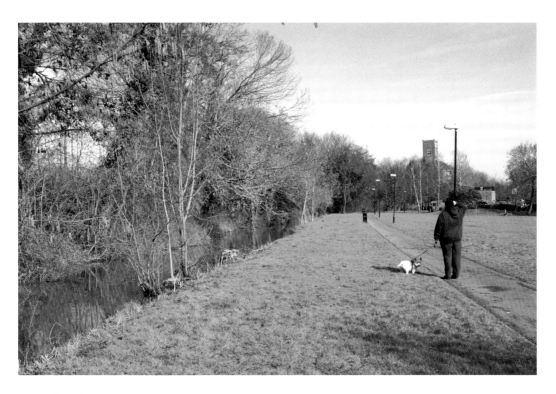

The River Stour

The River Stour and Lesser Stour flow along the southern lowlands near Ashford's town centre. Occasionally, at times of heavy rainfall, their banks can burst and water flows into nearby roads.

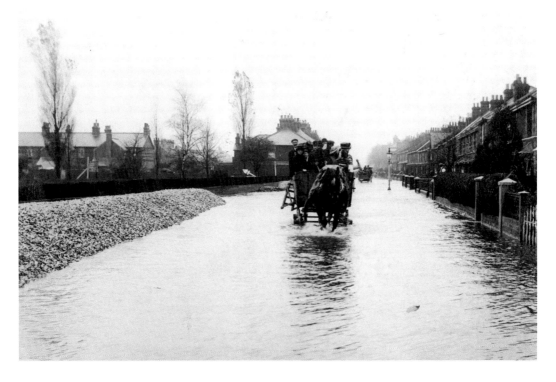

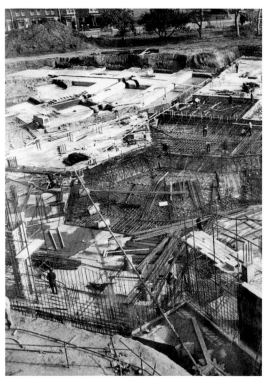

Charter Consolidated Office Block

A tremendous row over the planned erection of Charter Consolidated's giant office block raged in the late 1960s and early 1970s. Despite employment advantages its incongruous emergence above medieval rooftops even now strikes one as being totally out of context with its surroundings. Conservation at Ashford has, sadly, often been slaughtered on an altar of sweeping changes to whims of town planners.

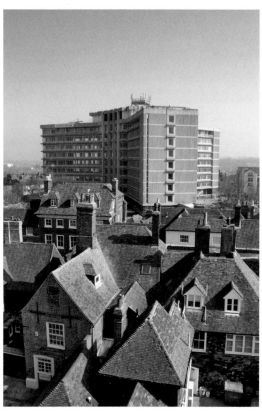

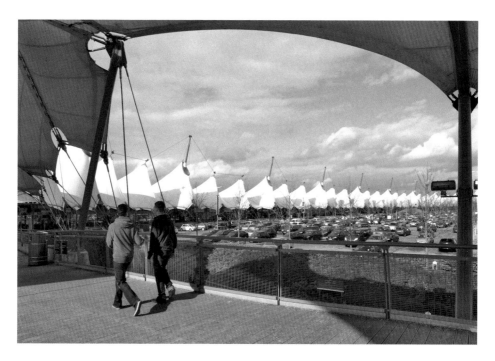

Designer Outlet Centre Ashford

Rightly awarded acclaimed architectural prizes for its concept and execution, this shopping mall was placed near to railway connections to take advantage of home and Continental demands. The simple idea of placing a car park in the middle of a circle of shops like a stockade mirrors the ancient town square concept and in this age of virtual universal car ownership explains graphically why conventional high streets are in terminal decline. Approached from the west, the plastic-coated roofline looks like a Bedouin encampment.

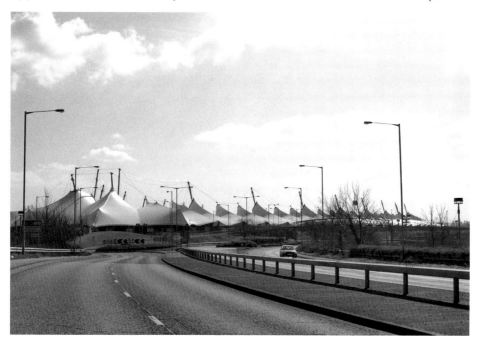

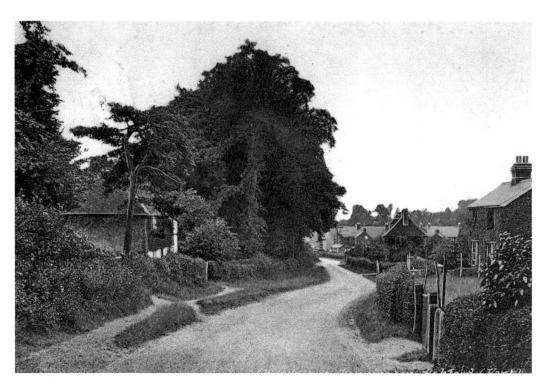

Church Road Kennington
Despite convergence with Ashford, parts of Kennington retain a rural landscape. Tucked away in hidden lanes and byways are a surprising variety of period cottages.

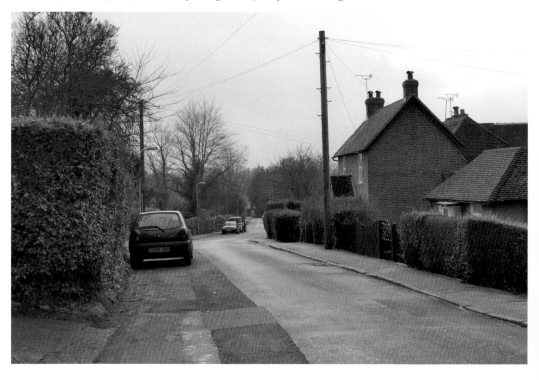

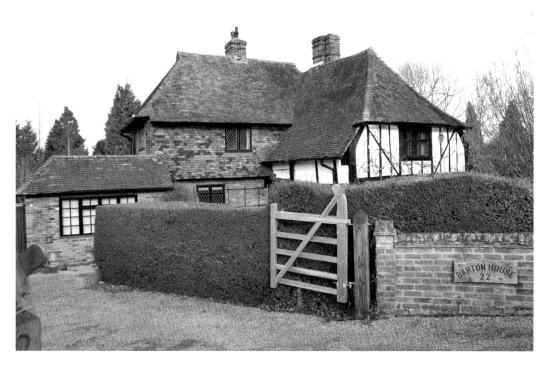

Kennington Cottages

After much searching it became impossible to identify the lovely old cottage depicted below on an Edwardian postcard. However, one of the best examples of pristine period properties that were encountered during the quest was Barton House pictured in the austerity of late winter.

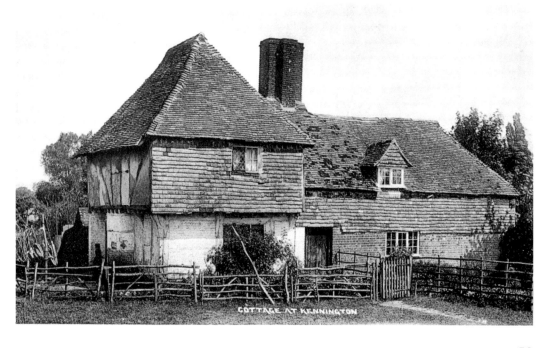

COTTAGE AT KENNINGTON

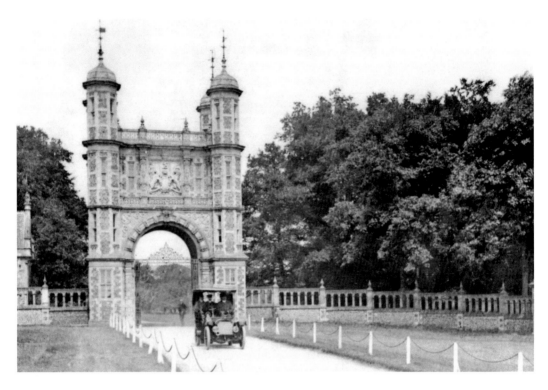

Eastwell House I

This peerlessly magnificent entrance gate to Eastwell Manor dates from 1848 when it was owned by the Earl of Winchilsea. By 1870 the 11th Earl had become bankrupt and the house eventually became the home of Queen Victoria's second son, the Duke of Edinburgh. Demolished and rebuilt in 1926, it is now a country house hotel.

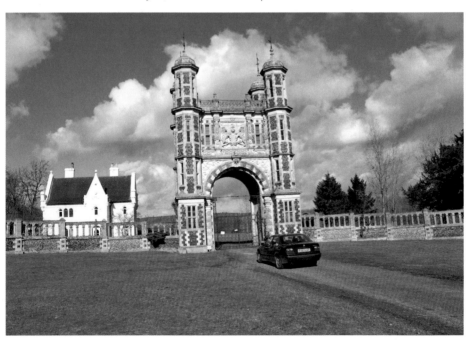

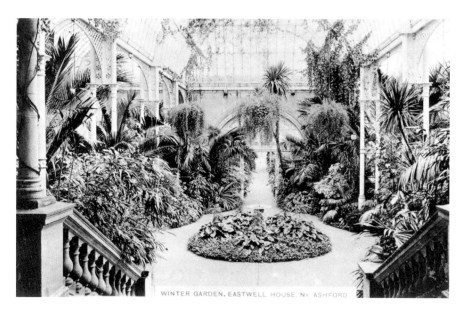

WINTER GARDEN. EASTWELL HOUSE. Nr ASHFORD

Eastwell Manor II

Gardens and parklands surrounding Eastwell Manor add to the splendour and stately grandeur of this impressive pile.

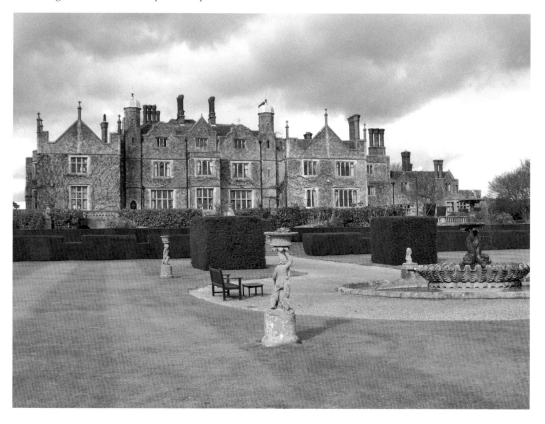

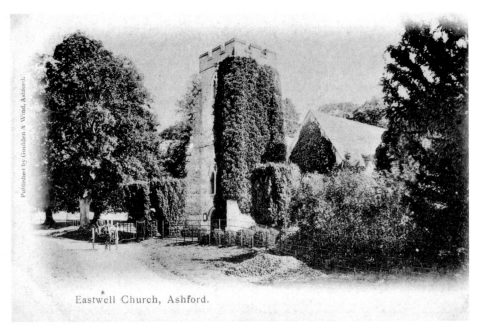

Published by Goulden & Wind, Ashford.

Eastwell Church, Ashford.

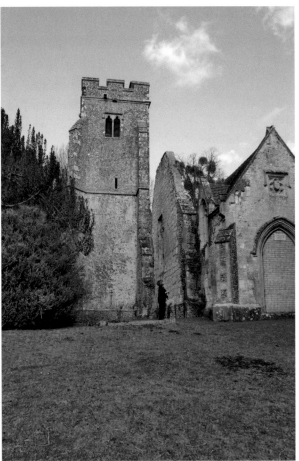

Ruined Church of St Mary's Eastwell

Tucked away on the Eastwell estate near the lake is the remains of Eastwell parish church. Its roof collapsed in 1951 and five years later further demolition took place to make the site safe. Within its churchyard there is a memorial to Richard Plantagenet, said to be son of Richard III.

H. E. Bates of Little Chart

This consummate wordsmith, short story writer and novelist moved from his home town in Northamptonshire to make his home at Little Chart. His love of nature, gardening and country folk was often reflected in his vast array of published work. Perhaps he will be best remembered for his tale of the irrepressibly happy yet roguish Larkin family in *The Darling Buds of May*. The televised version was shot on location in and around Pluckley and the Kent countryside which he grew to love so deeply.

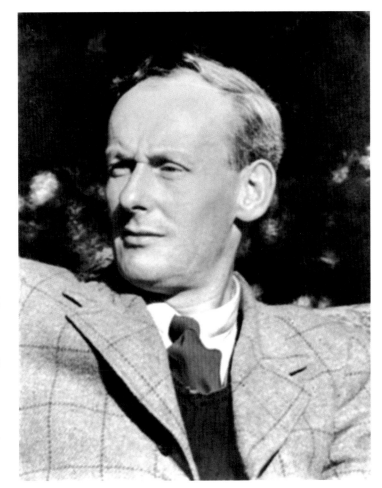

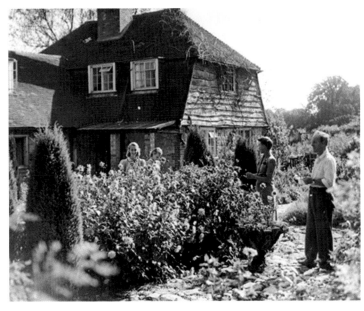

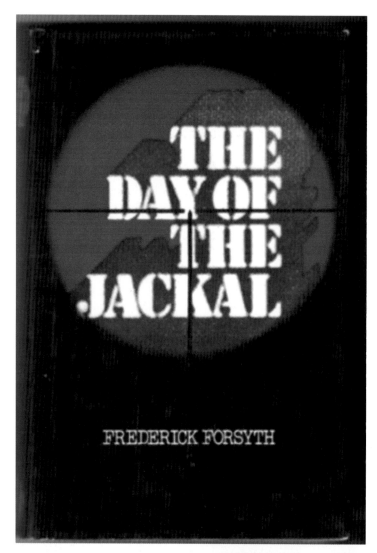

Freddie Forsyth a Son of Ashford

The famous author Freddie Forsyth was brought up by superlatively supportive parents who ran a furrier shop in Ashford. After attending probably Kent's finest school, Tonbridge, he embarked on a career as a journalist following service with the RAF. His first novel, *The Day of the Jackal*, was an instant success. A copy of the first edition's cover is shown here along with a portrait of the writer set against the backdrop of Paris where the enthralling plot of attempted assassination is played out.

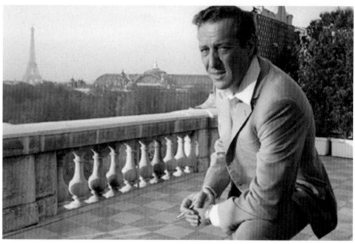

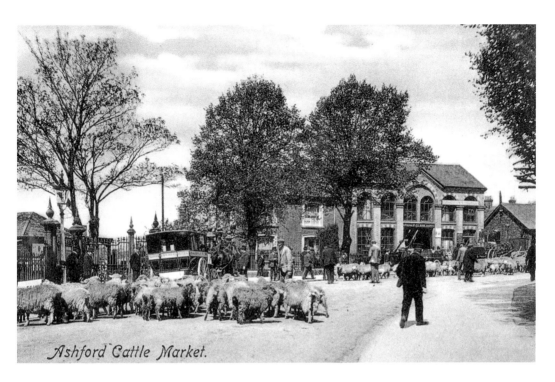

Ashford Cattle Market.

Ashford Market I

Close to the internationally renowned pastures of Romney Marsh, Ashford served as a convenient market centre for livestock. Today, it is still a major south-eastern trading forum for live cattle and sheep. Three phases of development have been made from the crude High Street venue to purpose-built pens off Elwick road (where its incorporation made it one of the oldest surviving corporations from the 1855 Companies Act) to its modern out-of-town location displayed below.

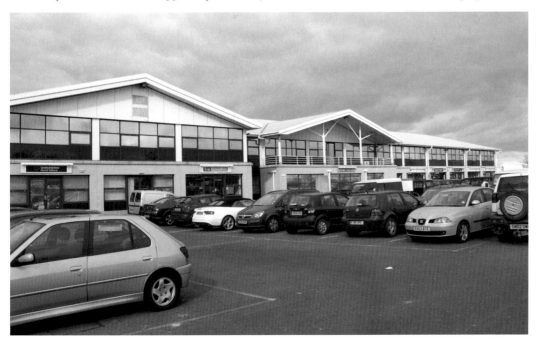

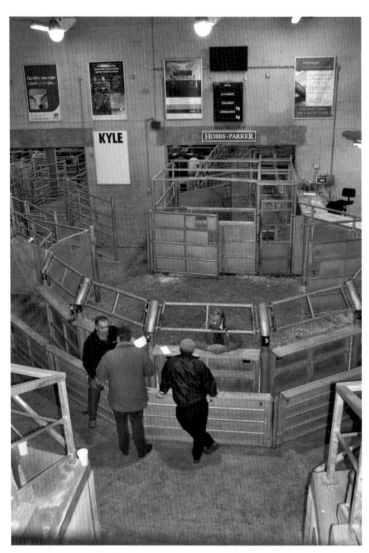

Ashford Market II
As much a social as
well as an economic
gathering, regular sales
provide a framework
for isolated farming
folk to come together
and gossip about
prices, neighbours and
any general banter that
takes their fancy.

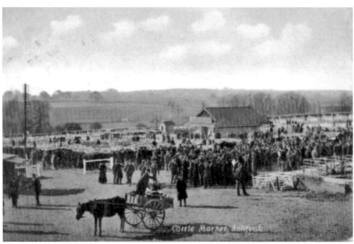

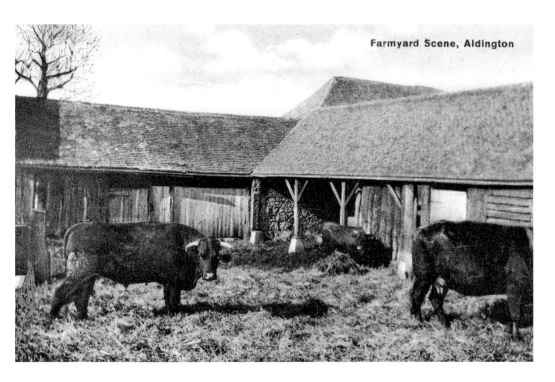

Farmyard Scene, Aldington

Ashford Market III

The traditional local Sussex breed of cattle in the above old farmyard scene at Aldington have not been dehorned. However, the snapshot of a recent auction below shows that it is now a general farming practice.

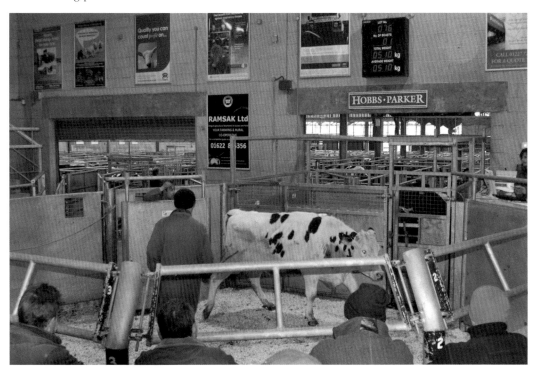

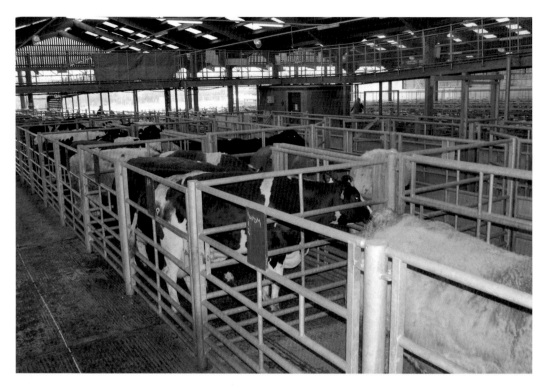

Ashford Market IV

Droving sheep to market was commonplace even up until the 1950s. The arcadian picture below illustrates shepherds with a flock of Kent or Romney breed on their journey to Ashford market from Tenterden.

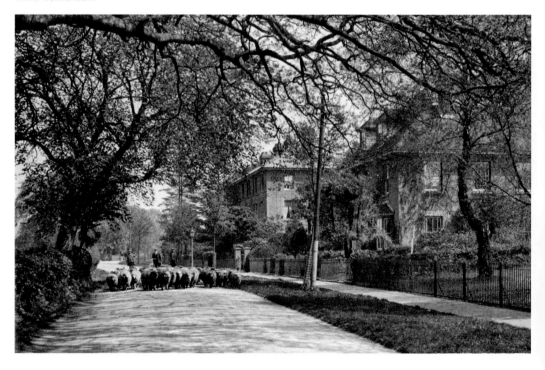

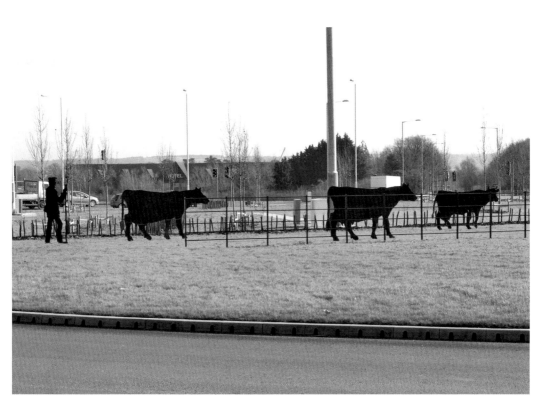

Ashford Market V

Unlike the concrete cows of Milton Keynes these silhouettes have some real significance and historical context for Ashford residents. However, few alive would remember when cows walked almost freely in the town like those less herded sacred beasts of India.

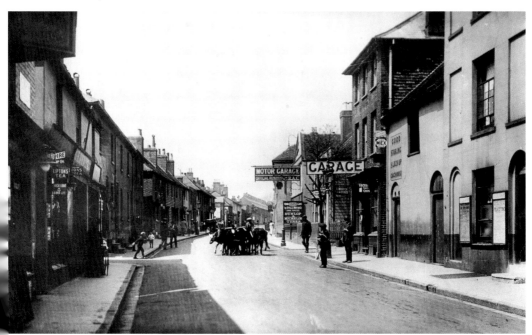

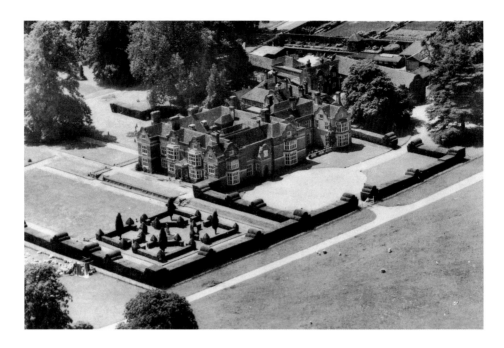

Goddington House

Near Ashford at Great Chart stands the incredibly attractive mansion of the Toke family for nearly half a millennium. Its mellow brick gables look out on neatly clipped hedges which repeat their arched shapes. It was here that Margaret Thatcher as Prime Minister signed the historic treaty which allowed for construction of the Channel Tunnel.

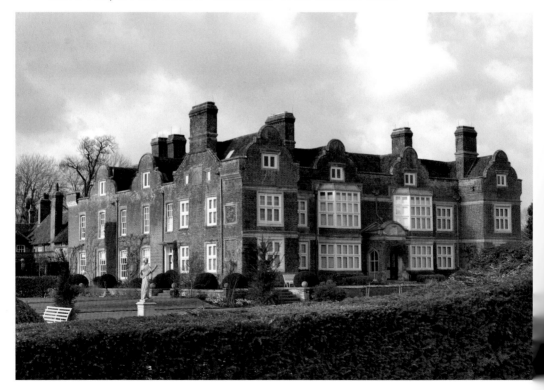

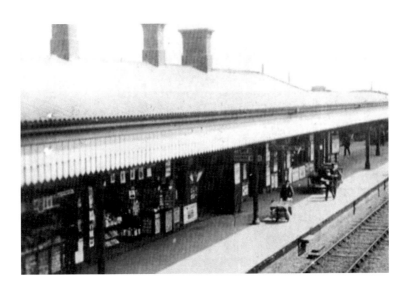

Ashford Railway Stations
The old Victorian railway station at Ashford is glimpsed above with its stout chimney stacks and willing platform porters pushing luggage barrows. Of a different age and futuristic style is the new International Station for high-speed trains shown below.

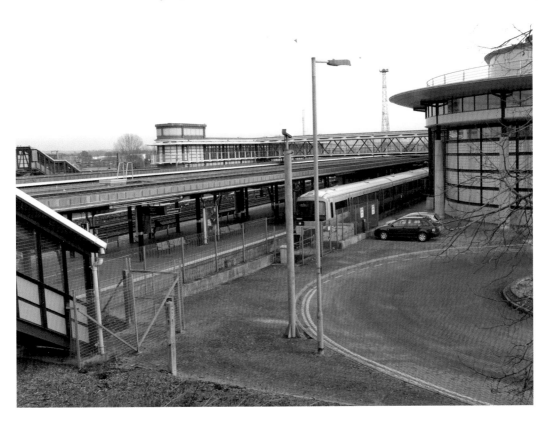

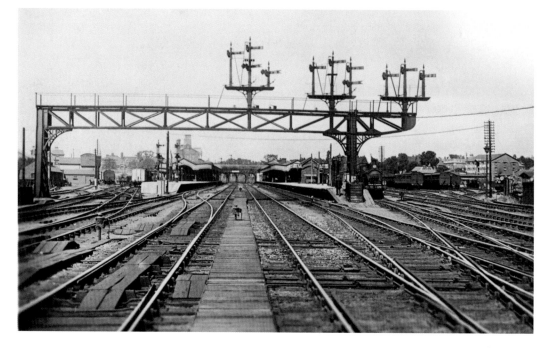

Tracks into Ashford

As picture compositions alone these scenes may lack visual appeal, but they do serve to illustrate how a large part of Ashford's *raison d'être* emerged. There have been five phases of track lying namely: (1) 1842–44 South Eastern railway line to Dover; (2) 1846 line to Margate and junction opened; (3) 1851 Marshlink to Hastings opened; (4) 1884 connection to Maidstone; (5) 1994 Channel Tunnel Eurostar trains on High Speed 1 line take trains to London in 37 minutes – a reduction of the previous time by 46 minutes.

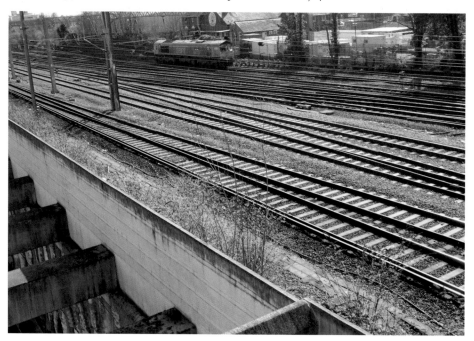

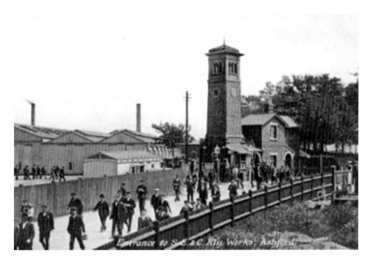

Railway Works I

In 1886 Black, in his *Guide to Kent*, described Ashford as having 'become the centre of an astonishing amount of life and labour, enterprise and activity'. Most of this description can be attributed to the Railway Works where steam locomotives, carriages and trucks were manufactured. Literally a new town (Newtown) sprang up to provide housing for the thousands of workers who often arrived from outside the area. The company in true Victorian paternalistic fashion built baths, schools and other social amenities. The picture above shows staff exiting the gates at the end of a shift and mercifully this industrial relic still survives extant.

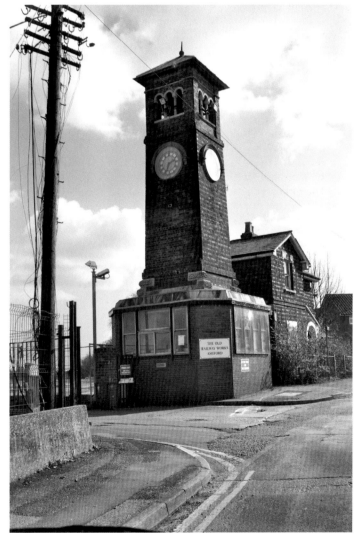

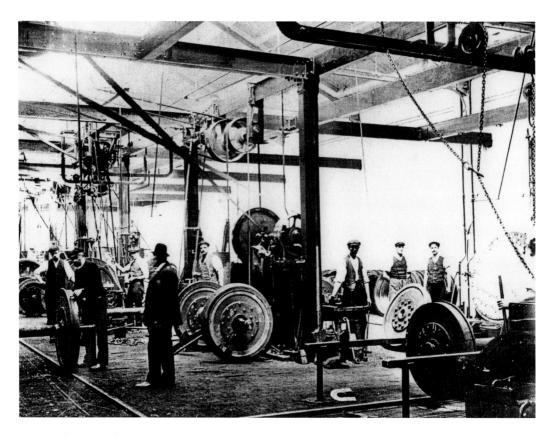

Railway Works II

These faded yet evocative photographs illustrate firstly the machine room where bogies where assembled and then how during the Second World War this factory suffered from being a vital target for German bombers.

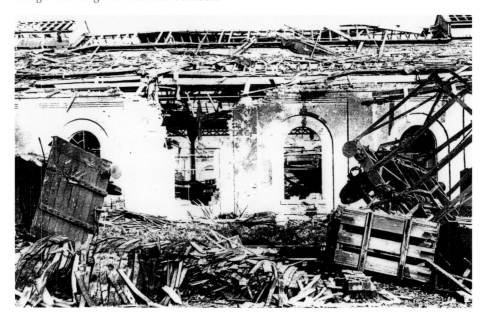

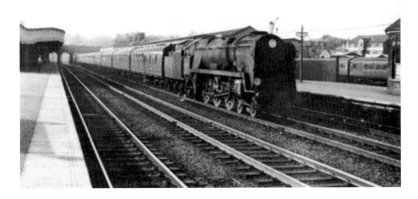

Steam Travel

Although just a dim distant memory for this author, steam locomotion was an integral part of the UK economy up until 1959 when coal was the country's main source of energy. The Duke and Duchess of York visited Ashford in 1926 and their tour could not be complete without an inspection of the vast Railway Works. The late Queen Mother to be is seen below standing on a loco footplate exhibiting her usual supportive role next to her nervous and courageous husband.

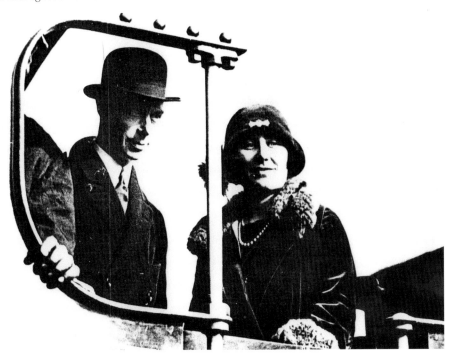

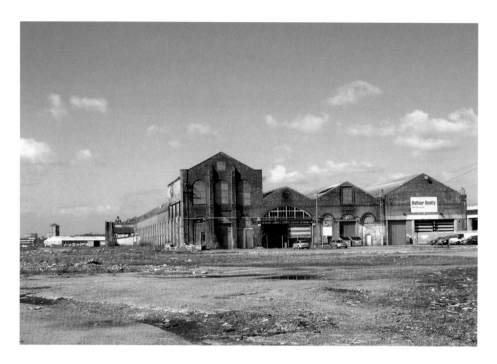

Railway Works Today

Reminiscent of Battersea Power station the gigantic buildings of the Railway Works have stood empty since closure in 1981. There is an eerie silence and emptiness to this site which once hummed with furious industrial activity. What fate or future use will await it? Will it remain in limbo, slowly deteriorating without anyone having the nerve to undo such a monument to human labour or will it transform into a new exiting future role? Only historians will be able to record the answers to these pointedly evaded current issues!

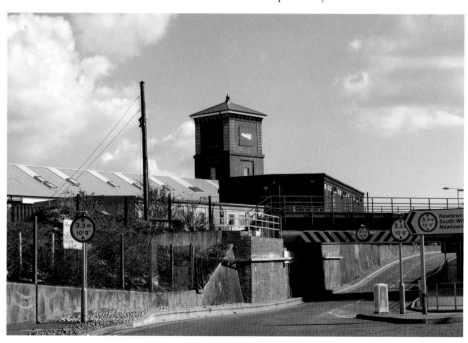

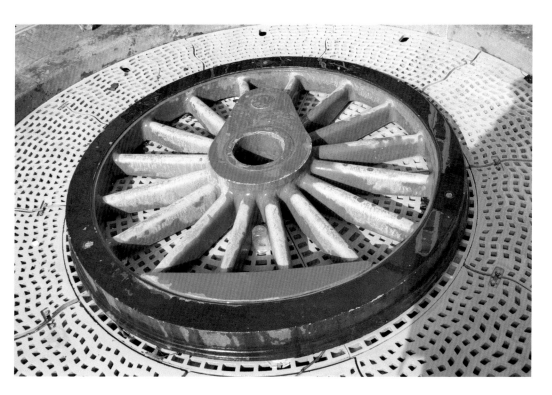

Train Wheel Fountain High Street

Cognisant of Ashford's historic links to the rail industry, authorities have installed an innovative fountain in the High Street. The pictures here show its details and setting in the urban landscape.

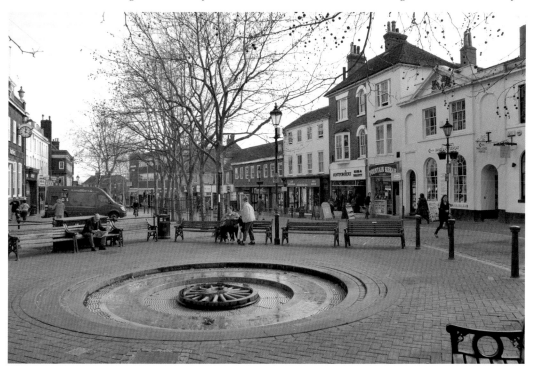

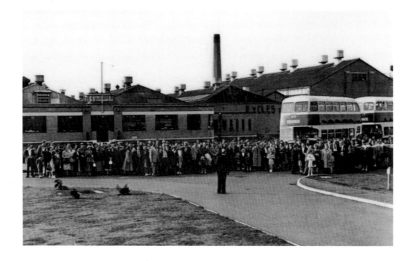

Norman Cycle and Motorbike Factory

From modest beginnings brothers Fred and Charles Norman developed a large firm making cycles and motorbikes. At its peak output was enormous with large export orders. Following retirement by its founders the business was taken over by Tube Investments who closed the works to concentrate on its more favoured original brand of Raleigh. The illustrations here show the workforce assembled for an outing and an advertisement for Norman Nippy. In fact, the Mark IV version was owned and used by this author forty-six years ago as his personal transport before he was old enough to drive a car.

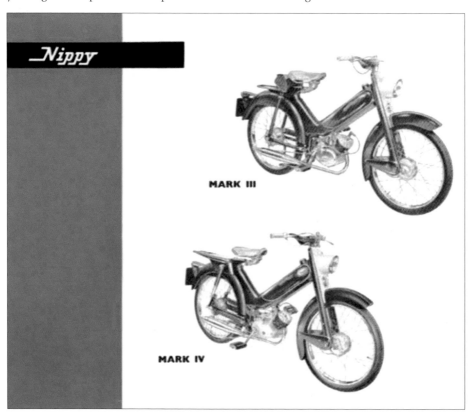

Nippy

MARK III

MARK IV

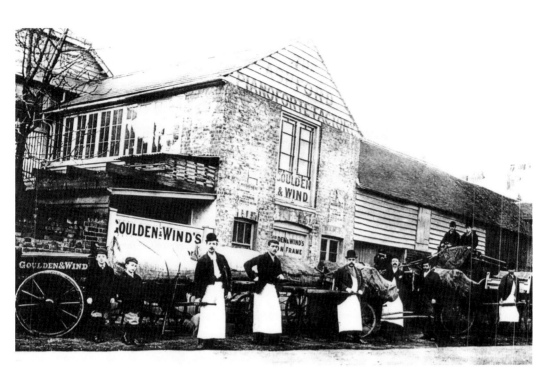

Specialist Makers of Ashford

Two old and unforgiving fuzzy images of unusual Ashford firms are displayed on this page. The first is of apron attired staff of pianoforte manufactures Goulden & Winds outside their premises. Below is a once exulted wheel maker – British Wheelwrights – who provided wooden wheels for vehicles ranging from modest barrows to royal state coaches.

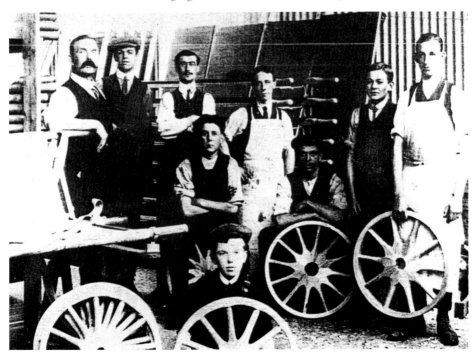

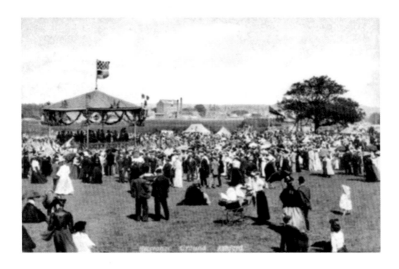

Recreation

In 1906 a recreation ground was opened and the populous festivities were focused on the bandstand above. Later Victoria Park gained the Hubert Fountain below when it was donated by local businessman George Harper after he had acquired it from Olantigh House, Wye, in 1911.

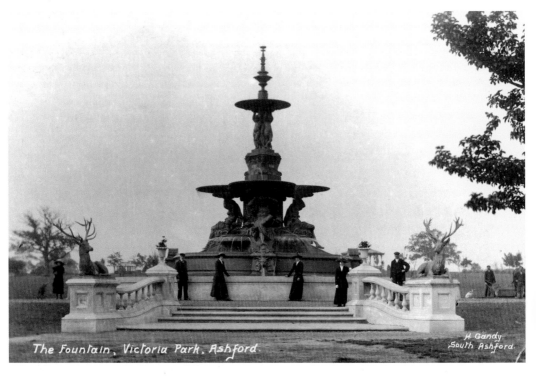

The Fountain, Victoria Park, Ashford.

H. Gandy.
South Ashford.

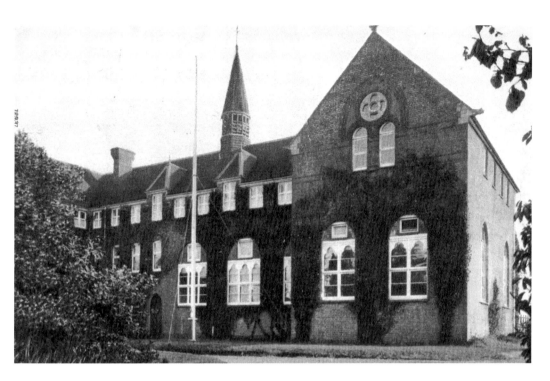

Ashford Schools I

With nineteen primary and six secondary schools only a small sample can be represented here. This page shows how Ashford Grammar School looked after Victorian relocation. The postcard of National Schools Ashford depicts mothers walking their offspring to class before the present trend of motoring there in 'people carriers'.

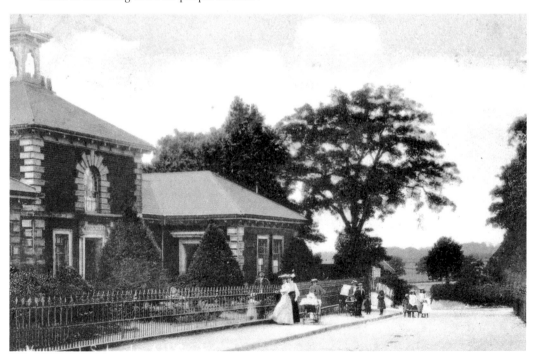

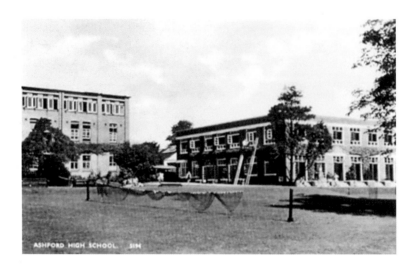

Ashford Schools II

Ashford school is this town's most prominent independent school. Founded in 1898 it occupies a large site near the Stour. Originally a girl's school it became totally co-educational in 2006. Academic and other standards are set high so the school has a well-earned reputation for excellence.

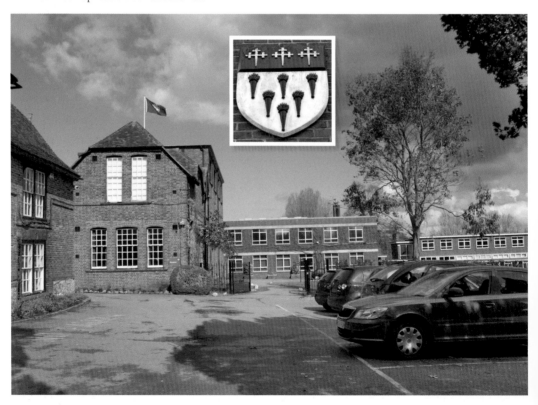

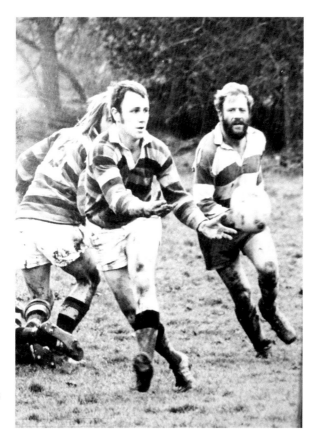

Ashford Rugby Club I

With over 800 members Ashford Rugby Club is a popular sporting venue. An air of purposeful relaxation pervades the present clubhouse pictured below, but teams have enjoyed the fun and games here since its formation in 1885.

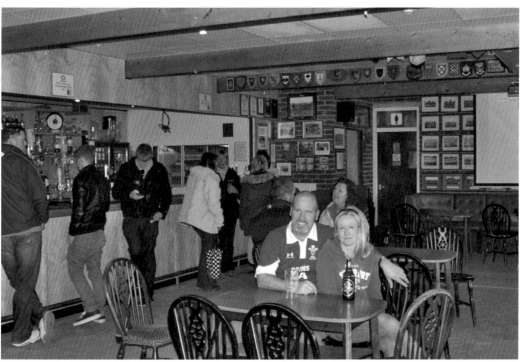

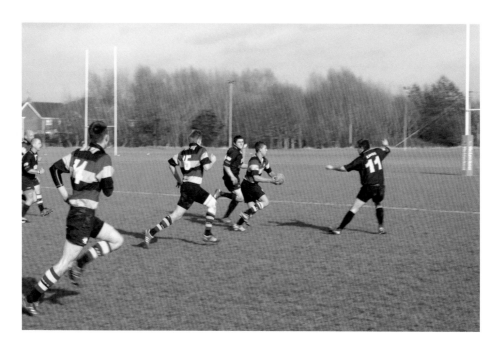

Ashford Rugby Club II

Currently Ashford Rugby Club runs four men's teams, a ladies' team and junior sides from under eighteen to under seven. The first team play in London & South East Division. The team photograph below of 1960 shows a smart sevens side with short hair and no beards or moustaches. Above, the three quarters line is in full flight against Deal and Bettshanger on 10 March 2012.

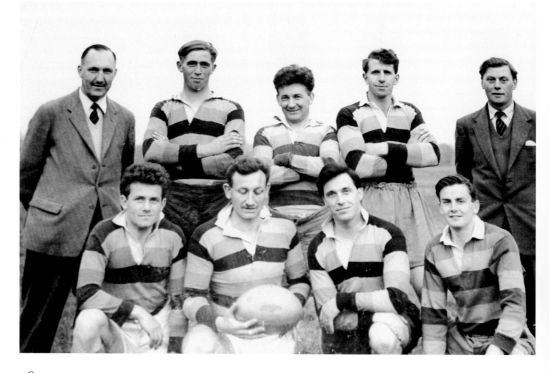

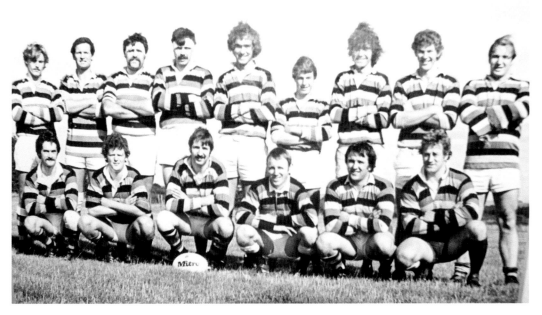

Ashford Rugby Club III

By 1979, longer hair and drooping moustaches have become the fashion for players as shown in the happy team line up above. The photograph below shows some of the present forward division performing in a lineout at the same occasion as pictured on page 78.

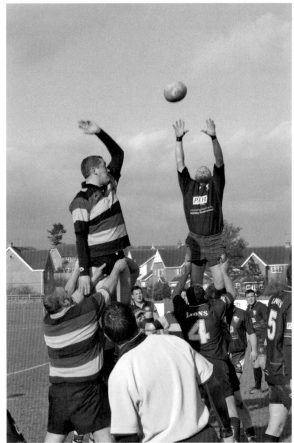

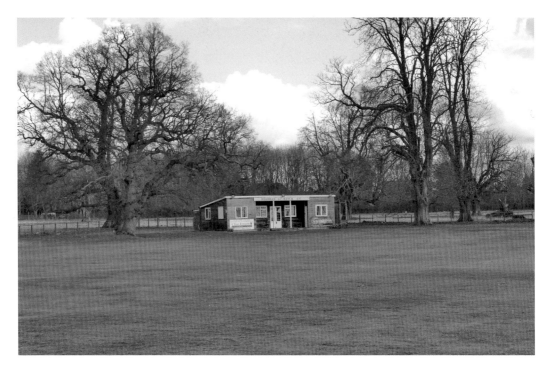

Cricket

Mersham Le Hatch is an arrestingly immaculate cricket club on the Hythe Road, Ashford. Its timbered grounds, where even royalty have played, are pictured above. Also the South Ashford team of 1924, stiffly posing for posterity below, probably played away here too.

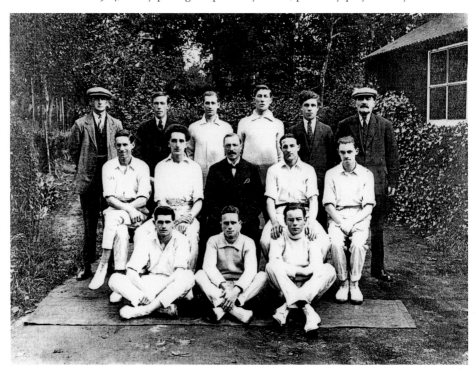

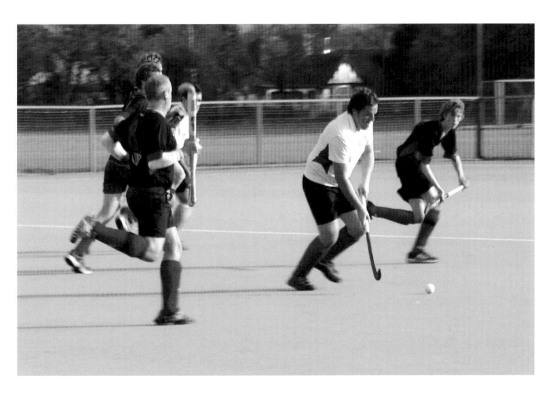

Ashford Hockey Club I

Ashford Hockey Club, who are based at Ball Lane, Kennington, run eight men's teams, four ladies' teams and numerous juniors. The picture above shows them in attack at their home ground on 10 March 2012. Below is an older ladies' first team portrait with universal smiles of success.

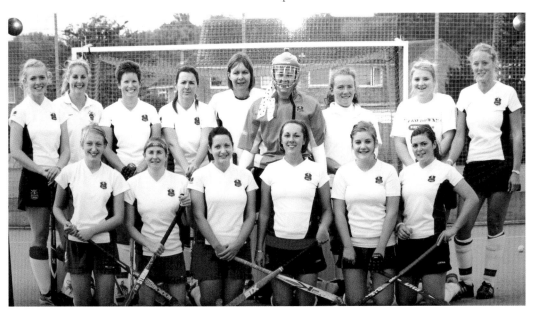

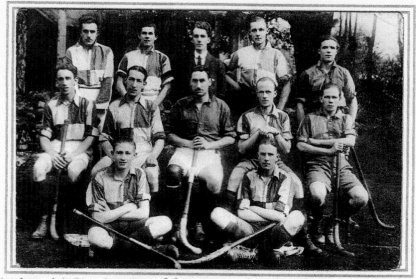

ASHFORD HOCKEY CLUB EARLY 1920s

BACK ROW: L. HOE: I. ROBINSON: F. GOODFELLOW: E. HOLE: J. FAGG
MIDDLE: F. HOLDSTOCK: A. GIBSON: D. PELLING: L. PREBBLE: P. HOLLEY
FRONT: G. WATTS: T. PREBBLE

Ashford Hockey Club II

The team photograph above was taken some ninety years ago, but the club continues to thrive attracting many spectators to its buzzing headquarters.

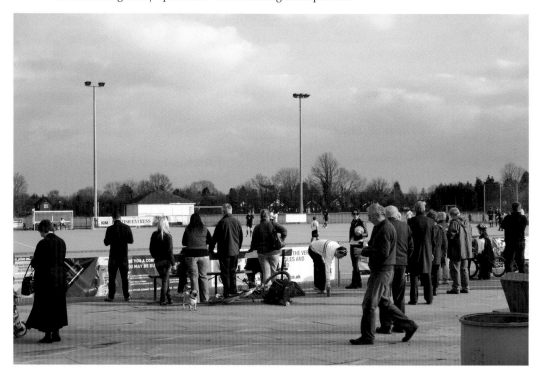

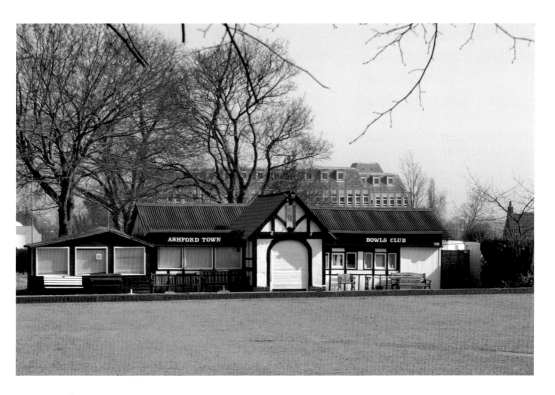

Bowling

For many years Ashford Bowls Club has been based at Church Road. A near neighbour is the indoor bowling alley with a much less traditional 'pavilion' below.

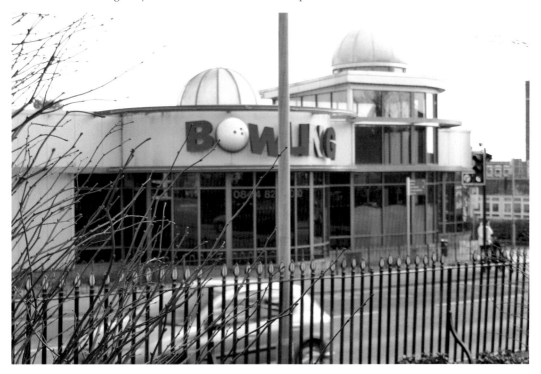

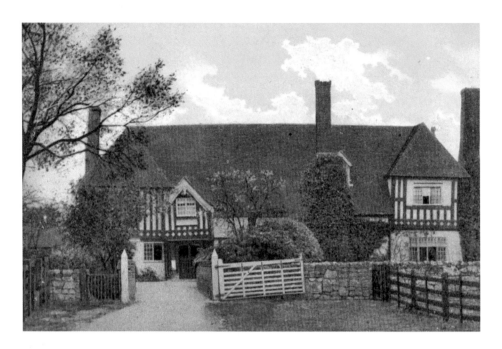

Singleton Manor

Located at Great Chart, and hidden away behind extensive modern development, is Singleton Manor with its surrounding moat. It is a venerable Grade II* listed building of architectural significance. Its present owners operate a small-scale bed and breakfast business. In the past it was the centre of a farming estate and the Engehems were the family responsible for its development from 1435–1603. Nearby a huge threshing barn that was once part of the outhouse complex has been converted into a public house.

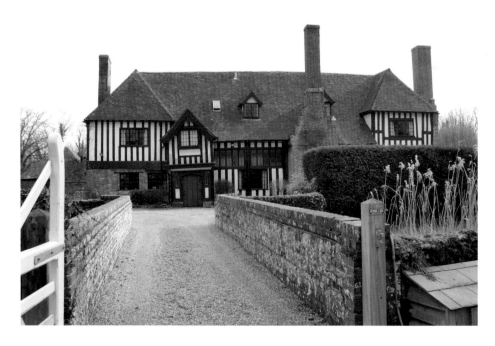

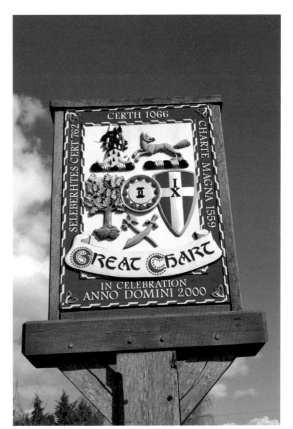

Great Chart I

The village of Great Chart is split between the ancient village pictured on this page and the modern housing development at Singleton. The church of St Mary is perched upon a ridge called Quarry Hills – so-called because of its stony outcrops. The rivers Stour and Medway run through the parish which is named after a Saxon family of Sybertes Chert (according to Ireland in his *History of Kent*).

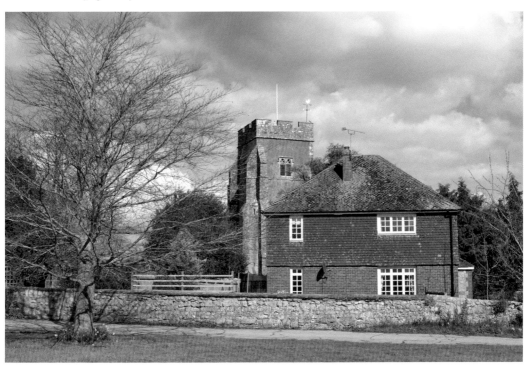

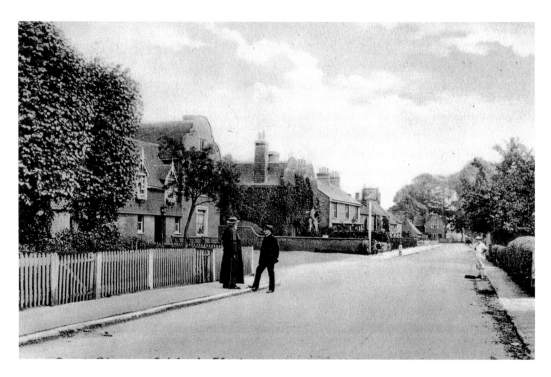

Great Chart II

The main street through Great Chart remains little changed over the past century except for the lines of parked cars. The community is served by two pubs and a particularly thriving cricket club.

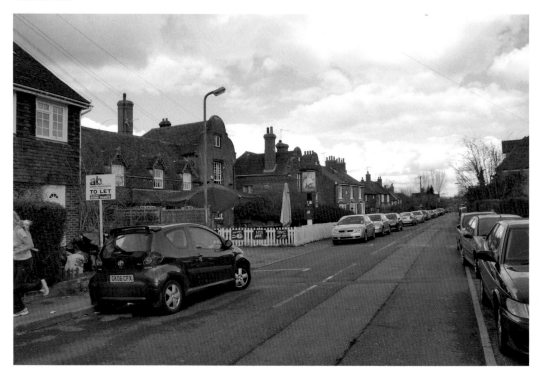

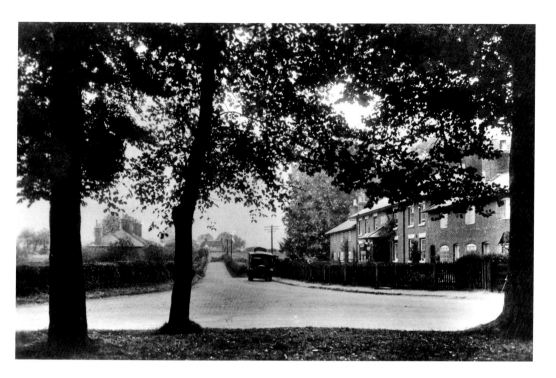

Hothfield

Hothfield is a village located north-west of Ashford with a nature reserve of some 143 acres. This common comprises heathland and lowland bogs managed by the Kent Wildlife Trust. These photographs of the street show how a quiet rural life is still preserved here, but there was some confusion over camera angle!

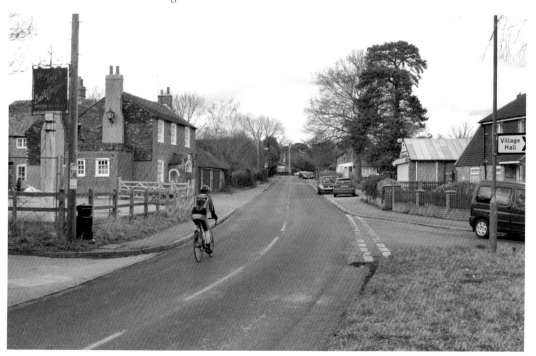

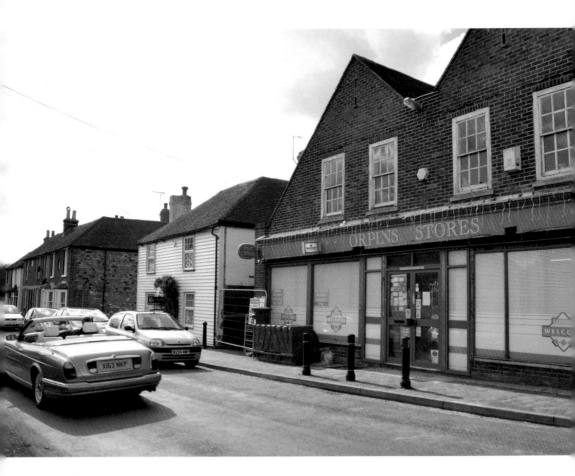

Smeeth

The village of Smeeth which derives its name from the Saxon 'smede' (a smooth open plain) confusingly occupies rather an elevated position looking southward into a valley. Back in the mist of time William de Baliol brother of King John of Scotland resided here at Scots Hall. Now it is an attractive friendly community with its post office relocated to the hub of activity.

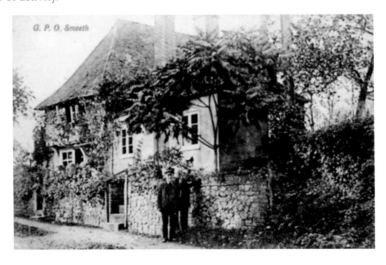

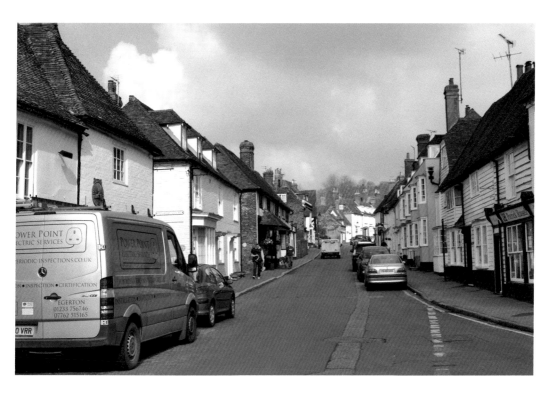

Charing

The street in Charing descends from the scarp face of the North Downs above Ashford. Always an important resting place for pilgrims and travellers alike, it is where Henry VIII lodged on his journey to the Cloth of Gold summit meeting in France. As was his usual preference he stayed in an Archbishop's Palace which exhibited a high level of luxury. Historic ruins of this building became used for farm storage and can be observed today.

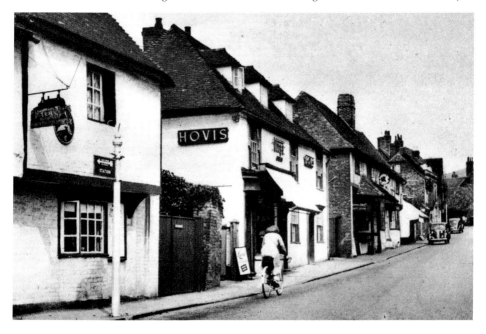

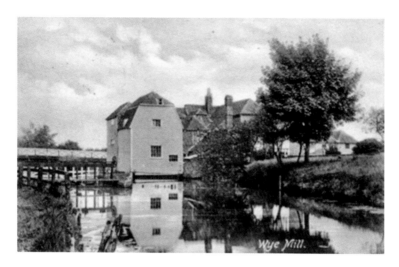

Wye I

The village of Wye developed at a strategically important point where a ford crossed the Great Stour River. A local lad, Archbishop Kemp, founded a college here in medieval times and parts of its structure are now incorporated into Imperial College's Wye campus. The pictures on this page show the handsome watermill near the railway station with only detailed fenestration alterations over the past century.

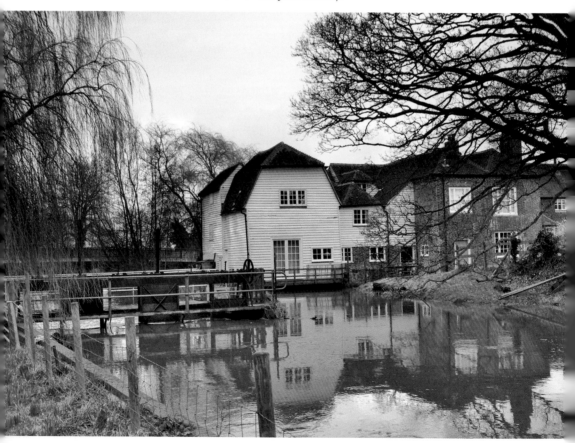

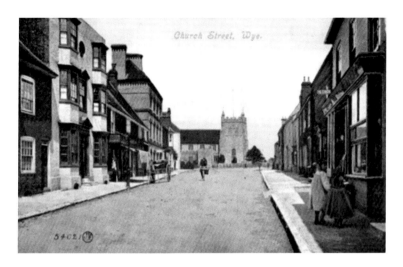

Wye II

Wye boasts many well maintained period properties and an excellent gourmet restaurant.
Its church originally endowed by Archbishop Kemp collapsed and was rebuilt in the early
eighteenth century.

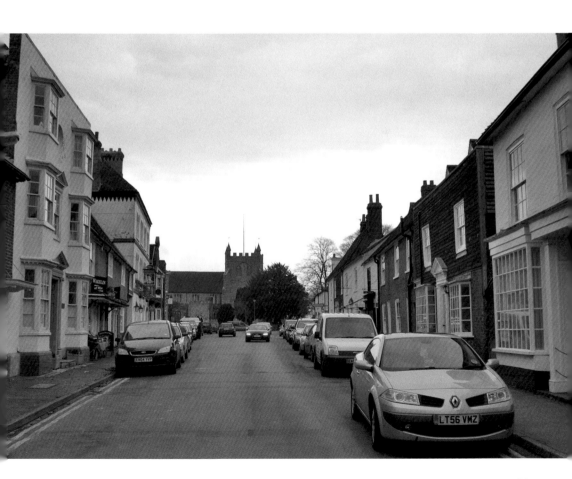

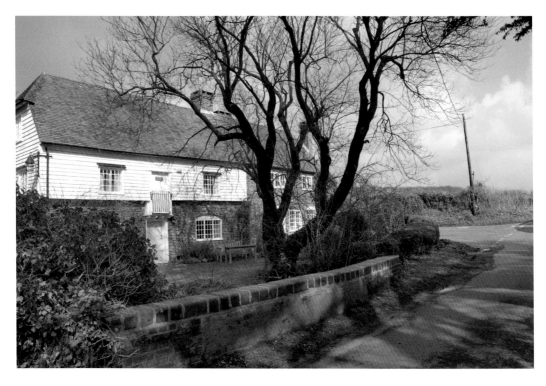

The Mill Westwell

Tucked away in exquisite countryside is this beautiful mill at Westwell. The structure is now wholly occupied as a dwelling, but the waterwheel is still attached to the west end which is from the sixteenth century. The former mill house is an eighteenth-century extension.

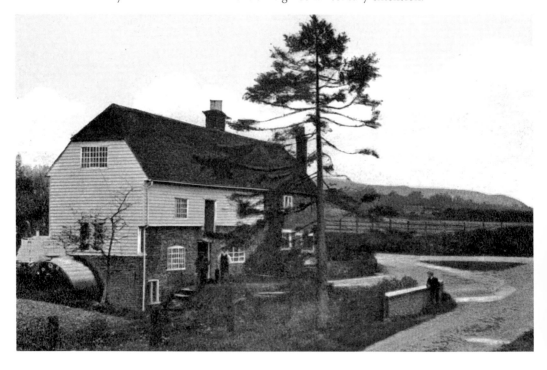

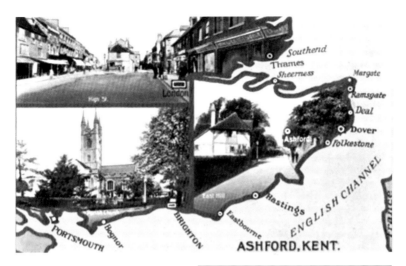

ASHFORD, KENT.

Tourist Souvenirs

As an important railway junction Ashford was visited by millions of holidaymakers on their journeys to either the Kent coast or the Continent. Like many travellers they were fond of buying small items to remember the places visited. Goss or crested china was a particular favourite along with ubiquitous postcards and perhaps even a discarded ginger beer bottle.

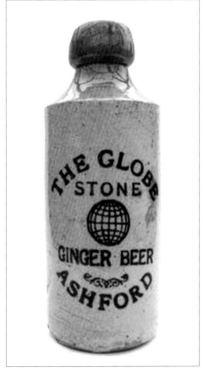

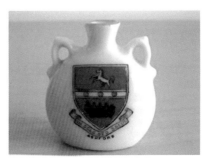

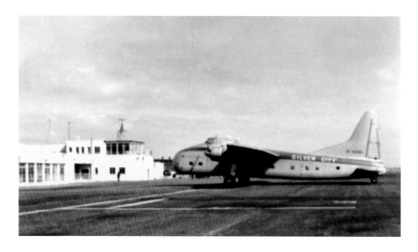

London Ashford Airport

Ashford was once served by Lympe Airport, but services ceased in 1974. However, the airport at Lydd was designated as London Ashford Airport although it is 17 miles away on the coast. Here regular flights to Le Touquet, France operate.

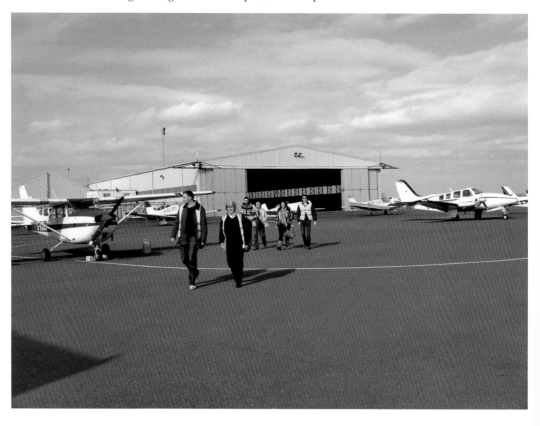

Acknowledgements

Firstly appreciation and thanks go to my faithful and beloved Jocelyn Watson who supported me with much patience and tact while operating the sattelite navigation during my exploits with camera in hand around the lovely countryside of Ashford. Thereafter, debts of gratitude are owed to Paul Whalen, Ian Thomas of Ashford Hockey Club, Chris Rapley and Trac Fordyce. Should I have failed, through any error of commission or omission, to include anyone who has contributed in anyway, I apologise and will naturally include their details in any subsequent reprint.

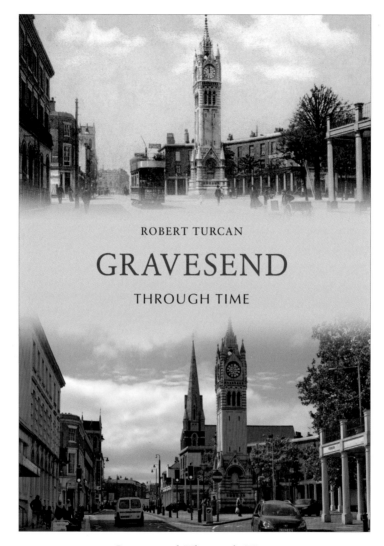

ROBERT TURCAN

GRAVESEND

THROUGH TIME

Gravesend Through Time

Robert Turcan

This fascinating selection of photographs traces some of the many ways in which Gravesend has changed and developed over the last century.

978 1 84868 125 5

96 pages, full colour

Available from all good bookshops or order direct from our website www.amberleybooks.com